AF207300

MAX-PLANCK-GESELLSCHAFT

Universität
Augsburg
University

TECHNISCHE
UNIVERSITÄT
MÜNCHEN

THE GEORGE
WASHINGTON
UNIVERSITY
WASHINGTON, DC

MIPLC Studies
Edited by

Prof. Dr. Christoph Ann, LL.M. (Duke Univ.)
Technical University of Munich (TUM)

Prof. Robert Brauneis
The George Washington University Law School

Prof. Dr. Josef Drexl, LL.M. (Berkeley)
Max Planck Institute for Innovation and Competition

Prof. Dr. Michael Kort
University of Augsburg

Prof. Dr. Thomas M.J. Möllers
University of Augsburg

Prof. Dr. Dres. h.c. Joseph Straus
Max Planck Institute for Innovation and Competition

Volume 28

Mikołaj Rogowski

Socialistic Brands

A Unique Category of Vintage Brands

Nomos

MIPLC Munich Augsburg
Intellectual München
Property Washington DC
Law Center

The Deutsche Nationalbibliothek lists this publication in the
Deutsche Nationalbibliografie; detailed bibliographic data
are available on the Internet at http://dnb.d-nb.de

a.t.: Munich, Munich Intellectual Property Law Center, Thesis "Master of Laws (LL.M.)" 2015

ISBN   978-3-8487-3548-8 (Print)
              978-3-8452-7881-0 (ePDF)

British Library Cataloguing-in-Publication Data
A catalogue record for this book is available from the British Library.

ISBN   978-3-8487-3548-8 (Print)
              978-3-8452-7881-0 (ePDF)

Library of Congress Cataloging-in-Publication Data
Rogowski, Mikołaj
Socialistic Brands
A Unique Category of Vintage Brands
Mikołaj Rogowski
85 p.
Includes bibliographic references.

ISBN   978-3-8487-3548-8 (Print)
              978-3-8452-7881-0 (ePDF)

1. Edition 2017
© Nomos Verlagsgesellschaft, Baden-Baden, Germany 2017. Printed and bound in Germany.

This work is subject to copyright. All rights reserved. No part of this publication may be reproduced or transmitted in any form or by any means, electronic or mechanical, including photocopying, recording, or any information storage or retrieval system, without prior permission in writing from the publishers. Under § 54 of the German Copyright Law where copies are made for other than private use a fee is payable to "Verwertungsgesellschaft Wort", Munich.

No responsibility for loss caused to any individual or organization acting on or refraining from action as a result of the material in this publication can be accepted by Nomos or the author.

For my parents *(moim rodzicom)* who've been there since the beginning; and for the other All My Friends who I've met since – you know who you are.

With special thanks to Prof. Ansgar Ohly for his kind support and confidence in this endeavour.

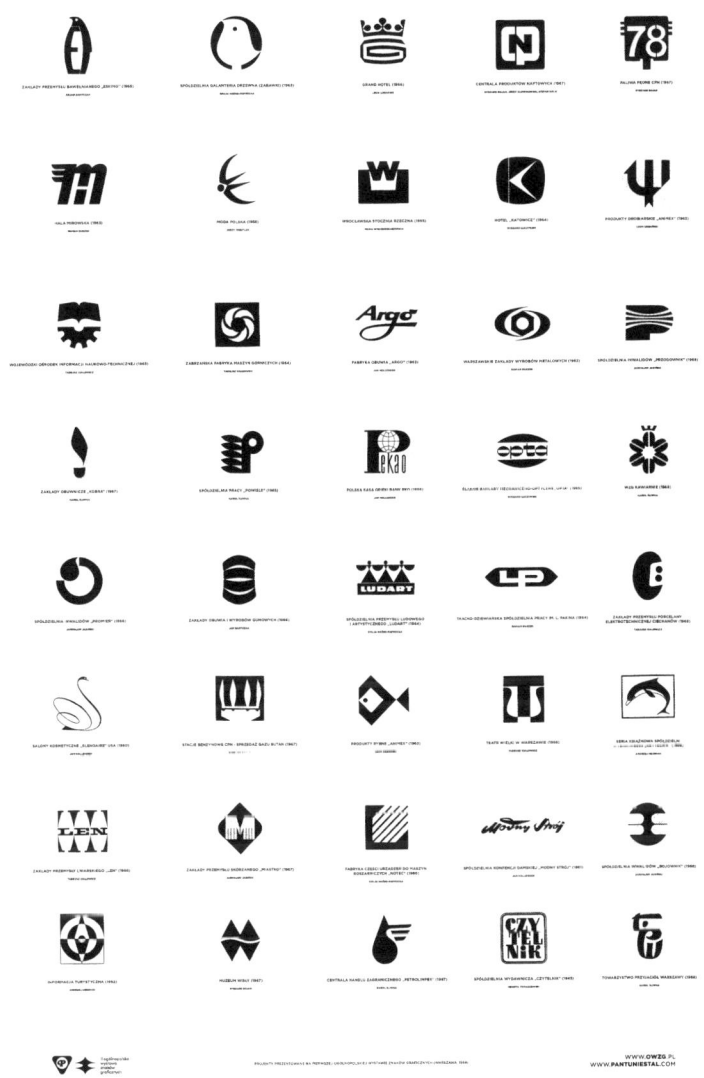

Poster of the Second National Exhibition of Graphic Signs (II Ogólnopolska Wystawa Znaków Graficznych), showcasing some of the designs of the Polish socialistic brands. Source/design: Pan Tu Nie Stał.

Mikołaj Rogowski

The author holds a master's degree in law from the Jagiellonian University (Kraków, Poland) where he is a Ph.D. candidate. He also studied in China, Italy, Sweden and Germany. Mikołaj wrote this thesis as part of his LL.M. in Intellectual Property and Competition Law at the Munich Intellectual Property Law Center where he serves as a member of the Alumni Advisory Board.

© Photo by Daniel Schäfer.

Abstract

Socialistic brands are a group of signs which were used within socialist countries by many separate actors within one territory and one industry, on various and inconsistent legal basis. A shared historical pedigree greatly influences the unique attractiveness of these brands within these territories. Their attractiveness is shaped by the particularities of bygone times, namely the socialist culture and the socialist market rules. Due to these circumstances, even years after the re-introduction of the forces of the free market, socialistic brands, due to their collective use, hold a particular place in the memories of post-socialist societies. This translates to their high value on the markets of the once socialist countries.

The analysis of the issues relating to socialistic brands has been conducted on the basis of a concrete example of a post-socialist country: The Republic of Poland. The basis of legal considerations of this topic was the European and Polish law and jurisprudence. Additionally, the author employs in his considerations findings from various branches of social sciences including semiotics, anthropology and social psychology.

Taking into the account the changing role of trademarks in the modern world and the unique attractiveness of socialistic brands, it is argued that public policy interests justify differential treatment of these signs. The author attempt to answer in which instances registering these signs as trademarks should be allowed and when such registration should not be permitted.

An assessment of existing trademark case law concerning socialistic brands shows that the current legal provision can be evoked against cases of unfair appropriation of this group of signs. However, analysed provisions do not constitute a satisfying mean of addressing the issue in a comprehensive way that would guarantee that abandoned socialistic brands remain out of the scope of trademark exclusivity. Having that in mind, certain solutions are proposed in order to help untangle the socialistic brands dilemma.

Table of Contents

Table of Pictures

Acronyms and Abbreviations

EUTMR	European Union Trade Mark Regulation
CJEU	The Court of Justice of the European Union (before 2009 Court of Justice of the European Communities)
EU	European Union
IP	Intellectual Property
IPA	Polish Industrial Property Act (Prawo Własności Przemysłowej)
NSA	Supreme Administrative Court (Najwyższy Sąd Administracyjny)
TMD	Trademark Directive
UCA	Polish Unfair Competition Act (Ustawa o Zwalczaniu Nieuczciwej Konkurencji)

I. Introduction

This dissertation is dedicated to the subject of socialistic brands, a specific group of vintage brands which share certain unique characteristics.

As the name of this group suggests, these brands were widely used within the territories of countries which belonged to the Eastern Bloc. Such brands were often used by many separate actors within one country and one industry, the legal basis of their use being various and inconsistent. This shared historical pedigree greatly influences the attractiveness of these brands within territories of post-socialist countries. This attractiveness was shaped by particularities which nations east of the iron curtain were subjected to, the socialist culture and the socialist market rules. Due to these circumstances, even years after the re-introduction of the forces of free market in these once socialist countries, socialistic brands hold a particular place in the collective memories of their societies. It could be argued that these unique cultural and commercial characteristics translate to unique attractiveness of these brands, which in turn might justify a call for an additional degree of protection of these signs from unfair appropriation. This thesis aims to determine whether that is the case.

The first section of this thesis sets forth a definition of socialistic brands and provides a justification for the choice of the scope of the consideration here presented. It also offers a selection of case studies of Polish socialistic brands in order to shed light on the specific characteristics of this group of signs.

The second part focuses on the consideration of whether socialistic brands possess characteristics affecting their attractiveness in the minds of consumers in such a far going manner that they should be treated differently than other signs. The author attempts to answer this question by employing in his considerations findings from various branches of social sciences, including semiotics, social psychology and anthropology.

The third section highlights legal problems at the core of which are the socialistic brands and aims to identify legal provisions which might be evoked against a specific type of behaviour which might constitute unfair appropriation of these signs. This part focuses on an analysis of the existing European and Polish law and case law in the area of trademarks whilst also briefly addressing other areas of law. Additionally, potential alternative legal means of protecting socialistic brands are outlined.

II. Definitions, the scope of the thesis and case studies of the socialist brands

A. Socialistic brands

Today, various fields of social sciences offer an abundance of definitions of the notion of the brand.[1] Classically, brands were defined as labels carrying meaning and association.[2] However, more recent, contemporary studies, which take into account dematerialization of these signs, tend to suggest that brands are a set of associations in the minds of the end users.[3] The changing role and nature of signs used to distinguish commodities plays a key role in consideration here presented.

For the purposes of defining the term 'socialistic brand' the notion of a brand should be understood as all signs that were used for the purpose of distinguishing commodities offered during the period of socialism within a territory of a given post-socialist country. This definition is necessarily broad and vague as it needs to encompass potentially all signs that were used as indicators of the source of goods or services, regardless of the basis and form in which the sign was used. The legal basis of the use of brands during the times of socialism were various and inconsistent. In some instances, these signs were registered as classical trademarks and later licensed to particular undertakings, in others they existed as collective trademarks. In certain other instances, various production units within a given country were eligible to use upon fulfilment of certain criteria. It was not uncommon for socialistic brands to be used by many partially separate actors belonging to the same large and concentrated industrial conglomerates, known as 'combines', functioning within one country and one commodity market.[4]

---

1 Paul Manning, "The Semiotics of Brand" (2010) The Annual Review of Anthropology 39, 34.
2 Philip Kotler, "Marketing Insights from A to Z" (John Wiley & Sons, Inc. 2003), 8.
3 Robert Moore, "From Genericide to Viral Marketing: On 'Brand" (2003) Language & Communication 23, 334.
4 A Polish example of this would be the Żołądkowa Gorzka wódka brand. Another particularly interesting instance of a situation created due to such circumstances

Socialistic brands were widely used within many states which were part of the Socialist Bloc, such as this author's home country of Poland. Each of the territories belonging to the socialist block has their own socialistic brands.[5]

During the period of socialism (1945-1989 with variations), in the states which embraced this ideology, the idea of prosperity was connected to the ideology of production. The identity of the citizens of these countries was embedded within state ideology, focusing on rituals of production and fetishizing physical, industrial labour.[6] The majority (if any) of competition between the undertakings was taking place in the form of bargaining for and procurement of materials.[7] Undertakings were deprioritizing the quality of commodities as the selling power of these was naturally high due to their constant scarcity.[8] Many socialistic brands had little competition on their relevant markets. Often they were among a very limited group of brands, or even the only brand, for which certain types of commodities were available.

The anticapitalistic and collective ideals of socialism played a fundamental role in the position these brands had and still have in the collective

---

was a dispute in the subject of rights to a Horalka Tatransky wafer brand. The dispute arose between an undertaking from Czech Republic and a Slovak one. Years after dissolution of Czechoslovakia both of these entities claimed rights to the brand. The dispute ended with a settlement. Parties agreed to tolerate others' use of the brand name as long as the graphic representation used on the packages are different (*See*: "Horalky Budú Vyrábať Opavia – LU aj I.D.C. Holding" (*finance.sk*, 12.4.2006) <http://www.finance.sk/spravy/finance/4993-horalky-budu-vyrabat-opavia-lu-aj-i-d-c-holding/>; "Dohoda o Používaní Názvu Horalka a Tatranka Více" (*Strategie.cz*, 8.11.2007) <http://strategie.e15.cz/zpravy/dohoda-o-pouzivani-nazvu-horalka-a-tatranka-443643>, both accessed on 27.5.2016).

5 Examples of such brands include the Slovak and Czech Horalka Tatransky wafer brand (supra n. 4), Russian Stolichnaya wódka brand, Hungarian Tisza Cipő streetwear brand and Romanian Arctic household appliance brand. For more examples *inter alia see*: Marta Karenova, "Soviet-Era Brands Rise On Socialist Nostalgia" (*Wall Street Journal* 15.11.2004), <http://www.wsj.com/articles/SB110046692372873477>;
Sergei Roganov, „Soviet Food Passes Taste Test for New Generation" (*Rossiyskaya Gazeta, Telegraph* 3.1.2013) < https://issuu.com/rbth/docs/2012_12_dt_all/8 > both accessed on 27.5.2016.

6 Daphne Berdahl, "'(N)Ostalgie' For The Present: Memory, Longing, and East German Things" (1999) 64 Ethnos 2, 193.

7 *Ibid* 194.

8 *Ibid* 198.

psyche of post-socialist societies. These ideals dictated many particularities. Separate units located in different geographical locations within a country belonging to collective socialist structures, offering the same types of commodities under identical brands. Even in cases in which one of these units would stop offering commodities, the others would likely continue their production. This factor, combined with limited space for private initiatives legally offering competing products, further affected the unique position socialistic brands had on the markets. In majority of cases end users' choice was reduced to what could be described as 'you either buy this or someone else will'. This in turn led to a creation of a prospering black markets. Black market trading of various branded goods made the commodities even scarcer and thus more sought after. Finally, as innovation and providing for consumer choice were of very low priority[9], many of the commodities remained literally unchanged through the socialist period, both with regards to their characteristics and their branding. This consistency strengthened the position of these brands even further.

Change only came after the fall of the iron curtain, which begun with the first partially free and democratic parliamentary elections in Poland in June 1989[10] and quickly gained momentum within the Socialist Bloc, culminating in the fall of the Berlin wall in November 1989. Many socialistic brands were abandoned in favour of new local or western brands.[11] Other socialistic brands, through various measures, held on to their market position.[12]

Today, both socialistic brands that were abandoned, either with the fall of socialism or in later years, and the ones which are still in use today, share common historical characteristics. They were in use for a substantial time period during socialism, functioned on the markets that offered little alternative combined with meagre or no incentives to change the branding or the commodities themselves. Markets in which extremely limited end user choice and availability of commodities strongly influenced their desirability. Because of these circumstances socialistic brands still

---

9 *Ibid* 194.
10 Inter alia: Norman Davis, "God's Playground: A History of Poland: 1795 to the Present (Volume 2)", (2nd edn, Oxford University Press 2005), 482.
11 Berdahl (*supra* n. 6), 195.
12 Examples of this would be the Żołądkowa Gorzka brand in Poland and the Horalka Tatransky brand in Czech Republic and Slovakia (*supra* n. 4).

strongly reside in the personal and collective memories of the post-socialist countries.[13]

By way of summary, the term socialistic brand, as used for the purposes of this thesis, should be understood as encompassing any sign that was used for the purpose of distinguishing goods or services offered for a substantial time during the period of the socialism. These signs share a historical pedigree of use in highly particular circumstances, which strongly affects the relation of these signs with the end users. These relations may be at the core of the attractiveness that socialistic brands evoke in the minds of end users within the territories these brands originated from.

B. *Geographical and legal focus*

The analysis of issues relating to socialistic brands is based on the example of a single post-socialism country: The Republic of Poland. This decision was based on a number of factors.

Firstly, Poland is characterised by a relatively big market and a population that makes it both the 6th most populous country in the European Union[14] (hereinafter: 'EU') and the most populous post-socialist country to have joined the community. These characteristic translate into a relatively high number of examples of socialistic brands.

Secondly, Poland became a member state of the EU during the first wave of accession of the post-socialist states in May 2004[15] and has fully implemented the framework of EU law regulating the area of intellectual property (hereinafter: 'IP'). This thesis was therefore able to benefit from over 10 years of post-accession jurisprudential and court experience. The fact that Poland is a part of the shared EU legal framework also makes the results of this dissertation applicable to other post-socialist countries which share this framework. As the result of this, auxiliary invocation of case law and examples from other EU members was possible.

Thirdly, Poland's borders have remained unchanged after the transformation. Polish territory was not subject to unification (as the territory of East Germany) or dissolution (as the territory of Czechoslovakia) which

---

13 Berdahl (*supra* n. 6), 203.
14 Official European Union profile of Poland <http://europa.eu/about-eu/countries/m ember-countries/poland/index_en.htm> accessed 27.5.2016.
15 *Ibid.*

limited the amount of potential factors needed to be analysed, allowing the author to focus on the most universal of these brands' characteristics.

Finally, the fact that Polish is this author's mother tongue helped facilitate access to various relevant materials.

This choice of primary focus means that the legal consideration presented herein is based on the Polish law and jurisprudence. Substantial parts of this national law implement EU law. As national law should be interpreted in line with EU law[16], the analysis includes the jurisprudence of the Court of Justice of the European Union (hereinafter: 'CJEU'). The analysis also encompasses the European Union Trade Mark Regulation[17] (hereinafter: 'EUTMR') and the jurisprudence on its basis. Even though this legal act is a separate body of law from the national law, it has been stressed by the CJEU on numerous occasions that the terms of both of the EU legal acts dedicated to the area of trademarks[18] are to be interpreted identically[19].

---

16 Inter alia: Case C- 106/89 *Marleasing SA v La Comercial* EU:C:1990:395, [1990] ECR I-4135, p. 8.

17 Council Regulation (EC) 207/2009/EC on the Community trade mark (codified version) [2009] OJ L78/1 as amended by Regulation (EU) 2015/2424 of the European Parliament and of the Council amending Council Regulation (EC) No 207/2009 on the Community trade mark and Commission Regulation (EC) No 2868/95 implementing Council Regulation (EC) No 40/94 on the Community trade mark, and repealing Commission Regulation (EC) No 2869/95 on the fees payable to the Office for Harmonization in the Internal Market (Trade Marks and Designs) [2015] OJ L 341.

18 These acts being the Council Directive (EU) 2015/2436 to approximate the laws of the Member States relating to trade marks (recast) [2015] OJ L 336, (hereinafter: 'TMD') and the EUTMR.

19 Inter alia: Case C-363/99 *Koninklijke KPN Nederland NV v. Benelux-Merkenbureau* EU:C:2004:86, [2004] ECR I-1619, p. 97; Case C-329/02 P *SAT. 1 Satelliten-Fernsehen GmbH v. OHIM* EU:C:2004:532, [2004] ECR I-08317, p. 26; Case C-320/12 *Malaysia Diary Industries Pte. Ltd v. Ankenaevnet for Petendter og Varemaerk* EU:C:2013:435, [2013] ECR I-0000, p. 35.

C. Socialistic Brands – case examples

To highlight the subject of this dissertation and to present the complexity of this area in a more comprehensive way, four of the Polish brands are presented below as case studies. They are referred to in the further parts, which is signalled by a presence of a graphical presentation of the brand on the side of the text, for easier navigation through the text.

1. Unitra[20]

 Unitra (a fanciful name) was a brand used for Polish produced and designed audio equipment. Products offered under the brand were mainly intended for export, their availability on the domestic Polish market was limited, and thus these products were particularly sought after. After the economic transformation following the collapse of the Eastern Bloc, all the unions and associations which manufactured the branded products were either dissolved or restructured. Until recently only few companies using the name Unitra existed, their activity limited to exports of non-Unitra branded products and real estate management. The audio equipment brand was re-launched in 2014. Today, the majority of the products offered are manufactured outside of Poland which, in accordance to the information provided by Unitra, is due to the company being unable to find the required production capabilities in Poland.[21] One of the products is a replica of the formerly produced headphones model Sn-50 which was one of the 'cult products' of the communist era in Poland.

---

20 Dawid Kosiński, „Unitra – Kultowa Polska Marka Powraca na Rynek i Oferuje Produkty "Born in Poland"" (*Spider's web*, 22.5.2014) <http://www.spidersweb.pl/2014/05/unitra-wraca-na-rynek.html> Unitra official page, <http://unitra.pl/>; Unitra club, <http://unitraklub.pl/unitra-dom> both accessed 26.9.2016.
21 *Ibid.*

pic. 1: An original advertisement of an Unitra radio set.

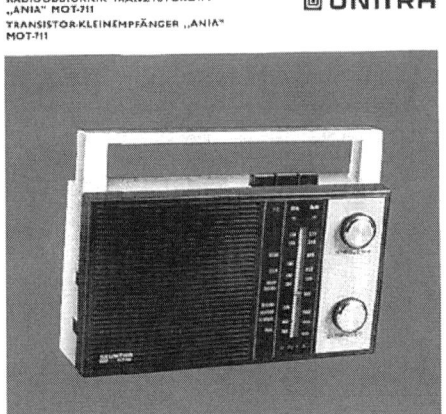

(source: http://www.oldradio.pl/foto_schematy/rekl00129.jpg)

pic. 2: Original Unitra Sn-50 headphones and their 2014 counterpart advertised by the producer as a "faithful replica".

(source: http://www.sklepunitra.pl/; http://olx.pl/oferta/sluchawki-unitra-sn50-orginaln
e-opakowanie-z-gwarancja-z-1975r-CID99-IDaMohh.html#a7499357c9)

2. Pewex[22]

 The internal export company Pewex (a fanciful name), founded in 1972, operated a national chain of stores, with products unavailable elsewhere. The products offered in Pewex, both imported and domestically produced, were highly sought after and were widely considered as status symbols. This exclusivity was further increased by the fact that Pewex shops accepted only foreign currencies. In 1980 Pewex was operating more than 1000 shops. After the fall of the iron curtain, due to mismanagement, Pewex gradually reduced its business activities, was subject to privatisation and finally filed for bankruptcy. The original Pewex trademark which was granted in 1974 was abandoned in 2006.[23] Pewex has been re-launched in 2013 as a web page Pewex.pl and subsequently the trademark was re-registered.[24] The web portal was initially dedicated to materials evoking nostalgia of the socialist era. Currently, it is primarily used as an e-commerce platform. The online shop offers a wide variety of products of other brands, including clothing, games and stationary, along with a line of clothing that is inspired by socialist times and uses the Pewex brand.

---

22 „Pewex Wraca na Rynek" (*Rzeczpospolita Ekonomia*, 16.12.2013) <http://www.ek onomia.rp.pl/artykul/1072971.html>; Ewa Cander-Karolewska, „Atlantyda Ludowa" (*Onet wiadomości*, 1.07.2007) <http://wiadomosci.onet.pl/prasa/atlantyd a-ludowa/dxxm3> both accessed 22.5.2016.

23 National no. of the right: 52219.

24 Grzegorz Marczak, „Dlaczego Chłopaki z Pruszcza Chcą Reaktywować Pewex? Na Moje Pytania Adpowiedział Sebastian Leśniak" (*Antyweb* 7.6.2013) <http://ant yweb.pl/dlaczego-chlopaki-z-pruszcza-chca-reaktywowac-pewex-na-moje-pytania -odpowiedzial-sebastian-lesniak/> accessed 26.5.2016.

pic. 3: *An original 1980s advertisement of Pewex stores from a weekly magazine "Motor".*

(source: http://bufetprl.com/2013/05/25/srodek-transportu-dla-wyjatkowych-towarow/)

pic. 4: *The main page of the Pewex.pl store with an advertisement of the 'citizen's collection' which includes clothing with the Pewex logo*

(source: http://www.ekonomia.rp.pl/galeria/706165,1,1072971.html#bigImage)

3. Herbapol[25]

Herbapol Herbapol ('herbata' means tea in Polish, 'pol' is a common abbreviation used to indicate the Polish origin) is a brand introduced by a state company group Zjednoczenie Przemysłu Zielarskiego Herbapol, founded in the late 1940s. Herbapol was the leading manufacturer of herbal food, health and beauty products in socialist Poland. After the referred earlier market transformation of the 1990s, the group was split and privatised. Currently there are five competing undertakings on the Polish market using the name Herbapol. In most instances the brand Herbapol is used along with geographical designations indicating where a given company is located. At present there are numerous trademarks registered with the Herbapol name including national and collective European Union trademarks.[26]

pic. 5: Primary logos used by each of the undertakings which currently operate under the Herbapol name.

source: http://www.herbapol.poznan.pl/; http://herbapol.pl/; www.herbapol.waw.pl; http://www.herbapol.com.pl/; http://herbapol.krakow.pl/)"

---

25 Herbapol Poznań < http://www.herbapol.poznan.pl/historia>; Herbapol Lublin < http://www.herbapol.com.pl/o-nas/kim-jestesmy>; Herbapol w Krakowie < http://herbapol.krakow.pl/o-firmie/historia>; Herbapol Warszawa <http://www.herbapol.waw.pl/>;Herbapol Wrocław < http://herbapol.pl/> all official pages accessed 26.5.2016.

26 OHIM no. of rights: 003868049; 003783016.

4. „Działka Moje Hobby" / Pan Tu Nie Stał

PTNS "Działka Moje Hobby" (which can be translated into 'allotment garden my hobby') is the title of one of the most re-printed books of the socialist period in Poland. Gardening and other recreational activities in allotment gardens were among the most popular ways of spending free time in socialist Poland, as many of state owned companies provided allotment gardens to their employees. The book was updated six times between 1977 and 1987 and had many editions and reprints including a translation into Slovak.[27] "Działka Moje Hobby" was never registered as a trademark, however its iconic cover designed by Jan Bok-iewicz is inseparably associated by many Poles with the time spent caring for the allotment gardens. The cover design has recently found its way onto one of the t-shirts offered by a Polish small-medium size clothing brand Pan Tu Nie Stał[28] which offers products inspired by, evoking and utilising the designs which can be associated with socialism. Pan Tu Nie Stał brand originated in the 21st century.

pic. 6: Cover of the book "Działka Moje Hobby" and the Pan Tu Nie Stał t-shirt using the same design.

(sources: http://pantuniestal.com/sklep/dzialka-moje-hobby-dla-pan/)

---

27 Results for "Działka Moje Hobby" in the Polish National Library catalogue <http:/ /katalogi.bn.org.pl/iii/encore/search/C__Sdzia> accessed 27.5.2016.
28 Could be translated as 'you sir, have not been queuing here'. A play of words that refers to an inseparable aspect of a purchase of any commodities in the times of socialism, namely waiting in immensely long ques whilst keeping a careful eye for anyone who would dare to cut the que.

III. Justification for the call for protection of socialistic brands from unfair appropriation

A. Introduction

A call for treating socialistic brands differently from normal signs is not per se impermissible, as trademark law already recognises groups of signs that are excluded from registration, such as certain shapes or official hallmarks[29].

However, it is more than reasonable to question why socialistic brands should be treated differently. It could be argued that because both the market and the perception of end users have been subject to immense and rapid changes since the fall of the iron curtain – and the transformations that took place after it – signs belonging to the group of socialistic brands simply do not carry any extensive selling power and do not possess other characteristics that would justify different treatment from that of other signs.

If anything, it could be contended whether socialistic brands might evoke attractiveness in end users other than the limited group consisting of users old enough to have experienced socialism themselves. It might also be contended that such associations (if any) have been greatly eroded by the ever rapid exchange of the information in the decades that followed the break-up of the socialist bloc. It could be added that the markets of the post-socialist period were dominated by end users showing strong preference towards the new brands. This in turn made the socialist heritage of brands an unnecessary aspect, devoid of any special economic value. What is more, it might be rightly pointed that many of the socialistic brands were associated with low quality and in fact carry negative connotations. This negative association might have been further strengthened during and after market transformation, as most of the state owned enterprises which were entitled to these brands were privatised, the survivors of this process being subject to turmoil as they were often unable to effectively compete in the free market economy. In other words, it could be

---

29 Art. 4(1)(h) TMD and art. 7(1)(h) EUTMR.

claimed that these brands have lost their distinctiveness and their re-registration should be allowed in order to save them from becoming generic.

All of the arguments presented above are considered and addressed in this section of the thesis. Socialistic brands were and are used to differentiate commodities affixed with them from other commodities. Having this in mind, the analysis of the justification of granting trademark protection is a natural first step in determining whether differential treatment of socialistic brands is justified. However, it should be kept in mind that trademarks do not exist in a vacuum. Trademark policy is more and more becoming a cultural policy.[30] Therefore, other areas of social sciences are also evoked.

B. Socialistic brands as signs used to distinguish commodities

1. Trademark law

Trademarks are signs used to distinguish commodities.[31] Their primary function is to indicate the source of commodities.[32] There are further functions of trademark that have been acknowledged in the jurisprudence of the CJEU.[33] It might be questioned whether legal protection of other functions of trademarks is justified[34] and if so to what extent, however it is unequivocal that in modern culture the role of trademarks goes far beyond

---

30 Burton Beebe, "The Semiotic Account of Trademark Doctrine and Trademark Culture", Graeme Dimwoodie, Mark Jamis (eds), *Trademark Law and Theory: A Handbook of Contemporary Research* (Cheltenham 2008), 59; Wolgang Sakulin, "Trademark Protection and Freedom of Expression: An Inquiry Into the Conflict Between Trademark Rights and Freedom of Expression Under European Law" (Kluwer Law International, 2011), 6.

31 Art. 3 TMD; art. 4 EUTMR.

32 P. (16) TMD.

33 Inter alia: Case C-487/07 *L'Oréal SA v. Bellure NV* EU:C:2009:378, [2009] ECR I-05185, p. 58.

34 Frank I. Schechter, "The Rational Basis of Trademark Protection" (1927) 40 Harv. Law Rev. 6, 813. It has however been argued that trademark law was not designed with an aim of providing protection of the per se commercial achievements of the producer (Inter alia: Martin Senftleben, "Bringing EU Trademark Protection Back Into Shape – Lessons to Learn From Keyword Advertising", < http://www.epip.eu /conferences/epip06/papers/Parallel%20Session%20Papers/SENFTLEBEN%20M artin.pdf> accessed 27.5.2016).

their source indicating function. Before we delve deeper into that territory, let us focus on the trademark law and the role it plays.

Trademarks are obtained through registration. An owner of a trademark right has the right to prevent others from using the mark in the course of trade.[35] The length of protection can be potentially extended indefinitely. This is justified by arguing that it leads to lowering the consumers search costs, by allowing the consumer to minimize the time she needs to search for a commodity characterized by certain qualities[36], thus positively affecting her decision processes by limiting the possibility of confusion[37]. The potentially infinite term of this exclusivity also serves as an incentive for the owner to invest in the quality of the product.[38] This in turn encourages competition between undertakings with regard to the qualities of the offered commodities. Undertakings are able to benefit from their previous actions by 'reaping' the goodwill and the attractiveness accumulated within the mark through previous actions.

In accordance to traditional trademark doctrine, uniqueness and differentiation of a trademark is gained through the use of it in its primary and essential origin function.[39] The value of the trademark lies in what could be described as 'its selling power'[40], its attractiveness. However, today trademarks themselves have become vehicles of values associated with commodities. Their attractiveness depends not only on the merits of the commodities but also on the uniqueness and singularity of the trademark, its psychological hold upon the public. This hold is acquired through action of the owner of a sign and end users' reactions to the sign and trademarks owners' conduct. This dialogic process[41] based on emotions of end users[42] also shapes the sign's uniqueness and differentiation from

---

35 Art. 10 TMD, art. 9 EUTMR.
36 William M. Landes & Richard A. Posner, "The Economics of Trademark Law" (1988), 78 The Trademark Reporter 3, 267.
37 George A. Akerlof, "The Market For 'Lemons': Quality Uncertainty and the Market Mechanism" (1970) 84 Quarterly Journal of Economics 3, 500.
38 *Ibid.*
39 Schechter (*supra* n. 34), 813.
40 Schechter (*supra* n. 34), 819.
41 Wolgang Sakulin (*supra* n. 30), 7; Martin Senftleben, „Trademark Law and the Public Domain" <http://papers.ssrn.com/sol3/papers.cfm?abstract_id=2280058> accessed 16.6.2016, 13.
42 Laura R. Bradford, "Trademark dilution and emotion" <http://papers.ssrn.com/sol 3/papers.cfm?abstract_id=1334925&download=yes> accessed 26.5.2016, 5.

other trademarks, which in turn translates to the economic value of a brand. Since trademarks carry rich layers of meaning and association[43] and thus play an essential role in social and cultural discourse[44], the uniqueness and differentiation of the trademarks should be understood as being shaped by a wide spectrum of emotions evoked in the minds of consumers[45]. Anthropological research, for example, indicates that trademarks serve as signatures of authenticity, showing that the commodity bearing it is true to its origin while at the same time they configure fidelity in another sense by registering a real contact, a moment of imprinting by the proprietor of the trademark.[46] Since trademarks function as figures of fidelity they also inspire fidelity in the minds of consumers, who endorse them by forming a bond with them.[47] A trademark, just as any other sign that evokes interest among end users, "is altered when the image one consumes is a mimetic version of one's self-when one's mass subjectivity, public subjectivity, and minority subject-position are conflictual"[48].

With the development of modern consumer culture, the market presence of actors to which the trademarks point has grown so much that in the majority of instances the proprietors of the trademarks are no longer natural persons but rather fictional, legal persons. Currently trademarks point not to a commodity's source but rather refer directly to the trademark. Trademarks should at least point to the goodwill associated with the source. This goodwill should function as a guarantee of quality, as the real source of the commodity is further obscured, in many instances to the extent that it becomes debatable whether trademarks in fact indicate any specific source.[49] In summary, many examples show that the attractiveness of a brand results primarily from the capacity of the mark to form a bond

---

43 Wolgang Sakulin (*supra* n. 30), 6; Johnathan E. Shroeder, "Brand Culture: Trade Marks, Marketing and Consumption" in L. Bently, Jennifer Davis & J.C. Ginsburg (eds) *Trademarks and Brands* (Cambridge 2008), 161.
44 Senftleben "Trademark law..." (*supra* n. 41), 13.
45 *Supra* n. 42.
46 Rosemary J. Coombe, "Embodied Trademarks: Mimesis and Alterity on American Commercial Frontiers" (1996) 11 Cultural Anthropology 2, 205.
47 *Ibid.*
48 *Ibid* 219.
49 Burton Beebe, "The semiotic analysis of trademark law" (2004) 51 UCLA Law Rev. 3, 646;Graeme Dinwoodie, "Reconceptualizing the Inherent Distinctiveness of Product Design Trade Dress" (1997) 75 North Carolina Law Review 2, 483.

with consumers and not the actual entity from which the commodity bearing a trademark originates.

As noted above, the justification for trademark protection is based on minimising consumer search costs and creating incentives for competition based on quality of commodities. However, consumer search costs are minimized only to the extent that a trademark actually refers to a product or source for which the end user is searching and the quality of product is enhanced only to the extent that the owner of a trademark attaches that trademark to products whose quality it actually controls.[50] Trademark owners' interest play a role in reducing the search costs only to the extent that they can be harnessed for the benefit of the consumer, namely to the extent the benefits of the goodwill encourage the mark owner to invest in quality.[51]

A grant of exclusivity to a sign should be limited to instances in which it encourages competition between undertakings on the ground of quality of the product, which translates to consumers associating the mark affixed on it with certain qualities.[52] In order to ensure such competition and limit the possibility of obtaining signs which would give an unfair advantage, trademark law envisages certain groups of signs that are excluded from trademark registration.[53] The question at hand ought to be if there is a public policy interest in limiting the possibility of registration of socialistic brands and if yes than to what extent. The registration of such sign will be unfair if it leads to confusion that deceives the end users[54] and thus does not lead to limiting the search costs, if it fails to create incentives to invest in the quality of commodities thus discouraging competition or if there are other reasons why a socialistic brand should not be a subject of trademark exclusivity. In order to determine this, we must first explore if socialistic brands possess a unique attractiveness that differentiates them from other signs.

---

50 Beebe, "The semiotic account...", (*supra* n. 30), 48.
51 Mark P. McKenna, "A consumer Decision-Making Theory of Trademark Law" (2012) 98 Virginia Law Review 1, 77.
52 Akerlof, (*supra* n. 37), 500.
53 *See* art. 4 TMD and art. 7 EUTMR.
54 McKenna (*supra* n. 51), 124.

2. Empirical evidence

The continuous presence of socialistic brands on the markets[55] might be evoked as evidence of their special attractiveness. However, it could be equally plausibly counter argued that these brands exist due to the efforts of their proprietors who used them after the fall of the iron curtain; that these brands prosper not because of but rather in spite of their heritage.

On the other hand, if socialistic brands possess no unique type of attractiveness how could one explain their re-registrations?[56] Why would undertakings prefer signs that could arguably be considered as aesthetically outdated instead of opting for new and more attractive signs?

  Re-launches of Pewex and Unitra and other vintage brands (practices of such re-launches are not limited to territories of the post-socialist countries[57]) could indicate that the registering undertakings believe that end users are attracted by these brands and the particular associations that they carry. As the business of the undertakings in the capitalistic markets is primarily centred on maximization of profits, it entails that these entities should act rationally, therefore at least some special selling power must exist. Strong interest in these signs is further proved by numerous legal disputes over the rights to these brands.[58]

Of course this evidence alone cannot be the basis of claims that the attractiveness of socialistic brands is different from that of other signs. However, it helps in identifying two main types of scenarios involving socialistic brands. The first one, a 'succession scenario', occurs in instances in which a socialistic brand has been or is being registered by a company that is a legal successor of the original state owned enterprise which was entitled to use the brand. The second type, an 'abandonment scenario', involves a fact pattern in which a socialistic brand is registered by a company that has no ties to the original state owned enterprise.

---

55 *Supra* n. 4, 4.

56 An extreme example of re-registrations is the case of an Armenian sweets manufacturer Grand Candy which seems to have based part of its business model on registering various socialistic brands as trademarks, including brands from other post-socialist territories (*See*: Դուֆ «Գրանդ քենդի» սա°ս էֆ սիրում (168 ժամ, 24.10.2015) <http://archive.168.am/am/articles/20366> accessed 26.5.2016.

57 Jerome Gilson, Anne Gilson LaLonde, "The Zombie Trademark: A Windfall and A Pitfall"(2006) 98 Trademark Reporter 6, 1280.

58 *See* part IV of this thesis.

In post-socialist societies it is common knowledge that the vast majority of the socialist state enterprises were subject to various transformations after the fall of the iron curtain.[59] Thus, in instances of 'succession' it is unlikely that the use of socialistic brands would result in confusion of consumers with regard to given commodities still being produced by the original state enterprises. However, in instances of 'abandonment scenarios' it is possible that some end users, due to the strong cultural meaning of these signs, could assume that the branded commodities are produced by a legal successor of the state entity. In addition to this there is also a risk, in both scenarios, that consumers could also be under the impression that the commodities are produced domestically or even in particular historical locations in which they used to be produced. At this point it should be noted that confusion with regards to the quality could affect choices of the consumers to a very limited extent as the socialistic products were often synonymous with low quality.[60] Since it is unlikely that consumer confusion will occur in 'succession' scenarios and because it only might occur in 'abandonment' scenarios in limited instances, potential confusion of consumers cannot be evoked as a sole justification of a call for differential treatment of socialistic brands.

The dominance of the so-called emotional branding in the contemporary marketing might help explain how the particular character of socialistic brands translates to their popularity among both the undertakings and end users. Today, the most successful commodities are the ones which manage to form a bond between the consumer and the commodity by engaging with the consumer's emotion.[61] That bond is more easily formed if brands possess a lasting history which translates to cultural connotations which resonate within the minds of consumers. Naturally, in order for the brand to acquire a genuine cultural connotation it needs to be used for an extensive period of time. This means that such unique meanings are highly sought after as forming them is highly time and resources consuming. For a proof of the value of cultural connotations, we need not look father than

---

59 On privatisation in Poland, inter alia: Piotr Kozarzewski, "Corporate Governance and Secondary Privatisation in Poland: Legal Framework and Changes in Ownership Structure" (Center for Social and Economic Research 2003) <http://ssrn.com/abstract=1443803> accessed 25.5.2016.

60 Berdahl (*supra* n. 6), 195.

61 Bradford (*supra* n. 45), 5; Also in general *see* Edward L. Bernays, "Biography of an Idea: Memoirs of Public Relations Counsel" (Simon and Schuster 1965).

at practices commonly employed by proprietors in order to evoke the history of the brand in the minds of the end users[62] such as the prominently used phrases like 'since' or 'established in'. Additionally, cultural connotations rooted in history make socialistic brands less prone to being affected by other circumstances that could affect the end user's preference. The attractiveness of such brands can be rebuilt by evoking their unique attractiveness rooted in their cultural connotations, for example through promoting 'coming back to the roots'.

In case of socialistic brands, the emotional bond of consumers, which is the core of their cultural connotations, is based on highly complex relation to the peculiarities of socialism and could be attributed to feeling of nostalgia, national sentiment, status of the purchaser or longing for a past that offers a national identity that no longer exists.[63] What differentiates socialistic brands from majority of other 'vintage' brands is that their cultural connotations did not result from the efforts of their owners but rather from their shared historical pedigree.

Socialistic brands were used as semantic links that pointed to the origin of the commodities, through utilising their commercial connotations. Both the cultural connotation and commercial connotation of the socialistic brands are subject to change. These changes will depend on the scale and other properties of the use of such brands.

For example, a use of the Unitra brand by its successors for the purposes of export services and real estate had a very limited effect on the cultural connotation of this sign and its limited commercial presence (as compared to the times of socialism) weakened its commercial connotation. Brand owners will naturally act to maintain or even strengthen the cultural connotation. Unlike the commercial connotations the cultural connotations are usually strengthened over time. However, it should be noted that since the cultural connotations of the socialistic brands spur from their commercial connotation, even in cases of abandoned brands both of these connotation will most likely remain strong.

As it is further shown in the section dedicated to semiotic analysis, in many instances continues use of certain socialistic brands or just references to socialism positively affect the preferences of the end users towards other socialistic brands. Abandoned or forgotten socialistic brand

---

62 For examples of such brands *see*: Matt Haig, "Brand Royalty: How the World's Top 100 Brands Thrive & Survive" (Kogan Page Publishers 2006).
63 Berdahl (*supra* n. 6), 195.

will remain in use through non-commercial communication. This could for example take form of a reference to past times in which consumption of one branded commodity was connected to the consumption of other branded commodities.

 An example of exploitation of this commercial effect of the cultural connotations was the two-stage lunch of the Pewex e-platform. Firstly, the domain pewex.pl[64] hosted a user-driven platform for sharing pictures connected to the times of socialism, including pictures of socialistic brands other than Pewex. Through this, the new owners of the Pewex brand were able to expand the brand's attractiveness before the launch of their core service. They accomplished this by employing an emotional branding strategy based on referring to nostalgic memories of socialistic brands through both user generated and edited content, both of which had the watermark 'pewex.pl' embedded into them. A less direct example would be the articles evoking brands associated with forgone times. Another example of exploiting the effect that the cultural connotations have on consumers comes in form of a retail strategy of one of the biggest Polish chains of supermarkets: Biedronka, which announced an assortment of vintage branded products.[65]

In some common law jurisdictions, it has been recognised that an ability of a trademark to identify the source of a commodity can reside in a sign long after branded commodities are no longer offered. The 'residual goodwill' is claimed to justify protection of such signs many years after the relevant trademark has been abandoned, as it is claimed that the use of such would cause damage to the previous owners.[66] Such reasoning has limited application to the case of socialistic brands. Firstly, because in almost all instances the socialistic producers of the commodities that were originally branded with such signs no longer exist in their original form. Secondly, the unique attractiveness of socialistic brands is anchored to their shared historical pedigree. It cannot be explained purely by pointing

---

64 Currently the platform is available at <http://retro.pewex.pl/> accessed 26.5.2016.

65 *See* official announcement of the launch of the vintage assortment <http://www.bi edronka.pl/pl/news,id,877,title,biedronka-zaprasza-w-podroz-sentymentalna-z-produktami-vintage> accessed 26.5.2016.

66 Valerie Brennan, T.J. Crane "Gone But Not Goodbye: Residual Goodwill in Abandoned U.S. Trademarks" (Inta Bulletin, 15.8.2015) <http://www.inta.org/INTABul letin/Pages/GoneButNotGoodbyeResidualGoodwillinAbandonedUSTrademarks.a spx> accessed on 26.5.2016.

to the goodwill, by evoking the reputation of the previous user of a trade-mark and the confidence of the repeat customers with regard to quality of the branded commodities. In many instances the commodities affixed with the signs were in fact of inferior quality. If their quality is fondly remembered it is mostly due to the nostalgic reproduction and falsification of the experiences of the past.[67]

The evidence presented in this part show that socialistic brands possess unique attractiveness that is attributed to their cultural connotations gained through their use in unique circumstances – their shared historical pedigree. However, in order to determine whether this unique characteristic justify a call for additional protection of these signs, a more thorough understanding of it is needed.

C. *Implications of semiotics*

Semiotics is a branch of social science dedicated to studying signs and their systems, investigating „the process and effects of the production and reproduction, reception and circulation of meaning in all forms, used by all kinds of agents of communication"[68]. For the purpose of semiotics a sign is defined as every object which in some respect or capacity has a meaning to somebody for something.[69] As trademarks are in their essence signs used to distinguish commodities, semiotics provides a wide variety of tools that can be employed in exploring the role and the boundaries of these signs.[70] Semiotics focuses on the sign nature of these concepts, not their legal status, thus the analysis presented below is applicable not only to trademarks but also to other signs used to distinguish commodities. However, highlighting the semiotic relevance of trademarks is not intended as a suggestion that the economic account of trademarks should be discarded in favour of the semiotic account[71]. Both of these accounts

---

67 Berdahl (*supra* n. 6), 202.
68 Beebe, "The Semiotic Account…" (*supra* n. 30), 261.
69 Charles Sanders Peirce in Charles Hartshorne and Paul Weiss (eds) "Collected Papers of Charles Sanders Peirce: Vol. II, Elements of Logic" (Belknap Press 1932), 228.
70 Beebe, "The Semiotic Account…" (*supra* n. 30), 43-44.
71 *Ibid.*

should be used complementarily, with semiotics being employed to guide us in filling the gaps in the economic account.

Trademarks, brands and other signs possess an internal structure.[72] A triadic mode introduced by Charles Sanders Pierce[73] seems to be intuitively suited for the purposes of explaining the semiotic structure of trademarks. It identifies three subsign elements: a signifier (which is the perceptible form of the sign, such as a word 'pen'), a signified (a meaning to which the signifier refers, such as the idea of a pen) and a referent (the tangible pen). In the realm of trademarks this translates to the perceptive form of the trademark being the signifier, attractiveness to which the trademarks refer to are signified and the commodity to which the mark refers is a referent. The elements of this system are mutually constitutive of and at the same time independent.[74] Users of the signs share a signified with other users through use (communication) of a signifier. The referent (the commodity itself) is the most stable of these elements as it belongs to the corporal world. The signifier (the brand, trademark) is less stable as it could be a combination of words, sounds or shapes that point to the meaning. Whilst the signified, the meaning (the attractiveness), will vary depending on many factors, including the circumstances of the use of the sign and the context of it. It is important to keep in mind that a sign is a system with relational characteristics and users can only perceive some element of this system.[75]

Today we are experiencing the breaking of the triadic structures of trademarks due to expansion of the scope of trademarks by actions of legislators, courts and the proprietors of the trademarks. This highly complex discourse[76] take many forms including enacting law, amending it, its interpretation as well as various actions of the trademark proprietors[77]. As any other discourse it "combines signs which have referents, of course, but these referents can be and are most often 'chimeras'" [78]. The widening of the scope of protection of trademarks, expansion of emotional branding

---

72 *Ibid*, 44.

73 Peirce (*supra* n. 69), 228.

74 Beebe, "The Semiotic Account..." (*supra* n. 30), 45.

75 *Ibid*, 45, *see* also: Jason Bosland, "The Culture of Trade Marks: An Alternative Cultural Theory Perspective" (2005) 10 Media & Arts Law Review 99.

76 *Ibid* 48, 49.

77 Jason Bosland, (*supra* n. 75), 7.

78 Roland Barthes & Richard Howard (tr) "Camera Lucida: Reflections on Photography" (Farrar, Straus and Giroux 1981), 73.

and the modern culture of consumption has led to a transformation of trademark system into a system in which signs no longer refer to commodities (referents), which are the primary subject of consumption, but rather to signs themselves.[79] An often evoked example of this trend is that of the Nike trademark. It no longer tells the end user where a product bearing it has been produced, who designed or who made it but rather suggest that the trademark itself produced the commodity[80]. The role the modern trademark plays in branding could be described as the role of obscuring the origin of the commodity, covering it over with a myth of the origin[81]. The origin function is obscured by layers of connotation which create a superior myth. In the case of the Nike brand, this myth consists of connotations of success or style. Socialistic brands are signs that naturally, due to their accumulated cultural connotations, communicate such a 'mythical' origin. It could be argued that this is very well the essence of the magnetism they have in the minds of end users.

If businesses can no longer rely on the strength of the commodities-referents, namely the qualities of the commodities offered, the focus naturally shifts to the 'chimeras', the signifieds. This translates into a strong preference or even necessity of obtaining signs with extensive magnetism. The more this magnetism is characterised by unique circumstances close to the end user the better. As trademarks no longer serve a role of lifeless symbols, they become autonomous, complex figures that in their own right carry with them relations of the end user to them[82]. Socialistic brands already possess such complex relations to end users, rooted in cultural connotations shaped by their use in the circumstances of socialism.

In order to determine if there is a need for additional protection of socialistic brands we need to investigate how their magnetism translates to trademark distinctiveness. Beebe employs semiotics in arguing that the trademark doctrine should recognise that trademark distinctiveness consist of two separate aspects. He identifies the 'source distinctiveness', which seems to mirror the concept of distinctiveness widely recognised in the trademark doctrine, and the 'differential distinctiveness', an extent in which a trademarks' signifier is distinctive from signifiers of other signs in

---

79 Burton Beebe, "The Semiotic Account..." (*supra* n. 30), 50.
80 Ibid 52; Paul Manning (*supra* n. 1), 45.
81 Burton Beebe, "The Semiotic Account..." (*supra* n. 30), 52.
82 Manning (*supra* n. 1), 45.

the trademark system[83]. Differential distinctiveness is based on Saussier's concept of value of a sign, in accordance to which sign value issues from the internal relations between the parts of the structure of the sign and other signs existing in the system.[84] This value of a sign is affected by varied circumstances. These include not only circumstances of how a given sign functions but also other existing signs, their value and the value of the groups they belong to.[85] This concept of value and the concept of differential distinctiveness offer a more comprehensive explanation of what constitutes magnetism of socialistic brands. A sign in most instances will increase its value the more often it is being used and the more unique that use it. During socialism, socialistic brands had usually little competition on their relevant markets, thus they held a strong position in the sign groups they belonged to, namely the brands of a given type of commodity and brands on the market in general. As they have been in use for a substantial time and in peculiar circumstances, which affected their connotations, they currently belong to many other groups. They exist not only as commercial signs but also as cultural signs. Due to these affiliations, these signs are still used today in movies, books and other cultural means. Furthermore, some of the socialistic brands, due to the scarcity of alternatives, were used so often in the daily socialist culture that in some instances they became synonymous with certain types of commodities. Another factor that affects the sign value of them was the limited access to the sources of information in socialism. The few media available were functioning under the watchful eye of the government, which made sure that socialistic brands were repeatedly praised, as they constituted an integral part of propaganda. All of this shows that because of their extensive use and a firm place in the memory of the post-socialist societies, today socialistic brands possess a unique level of differential distinctiveness accumulated in the cultural connotations they carry. The time factor also plays and important role as brands, which have acquired differential distinctness and have steadily kept it through time are more likely to retain it[86].

---

83 Beebe "The Semiotic Account…" (*supra* n. 30), 52.

84 Ferdinand de Saussure, Weds Baskins (tr.), Charles Bally and Albert Sechehaye (eds.) "Course in General Linguistics" (1966 McGraw-Hill Book Co), 112.

85 Beebe "The Semiotic Account…" (*supra* n. 30), 53.

86 Anne Meneley, "Time in a Bottle: The Uneasy Circulation of Palestinian Olive Oil" (2008) Middle East Reporter 248, <http://www.academia.edu/474517/Time_i

In contemporary practice, the main goal of any branding attempts of an undertaking is to establish, strengthen and stabilise associations in the minds of end users.[87] Socialistic brands offer a unique emotional link to the history of the post-socialist nations and since the access to the commodities in the socialist era was scarce they also carry certain positive connotation of the sought after signs of times gone by or identity that was stripped from the end users in the modern times.[88]

 A possible example of this unique magnetism can be found in the warm reception of the comeback of the Unitra brand, despite that arguably the old products of the Unitra could not rival the quality of craved imported west counterparts. Conclusions from the previous part find affirmation here. The majority of new trademarks could not possibly offer such a high degree of differential distinctiveness. In some aspects, efforts to compete with the socialistic brands would be futile, as their magnetism spurs from circumstances belonging to a historical era long gone. This limited availability of such signs with genuine socialist attributes further increases their differential distinctiveness.

Additionally, Beebe identifies a concept of 'sign value' which he describes as commercial magnetism, uniqueness, singularity and identity of the sign.[89] Beebe points out that this value differs from the economical and use sense of value. It is rather a "'commodities' differential value as against all other commodities, and thus the commodity's capacity to differentiate the consumer"[90].

The identity of the sign forms a particularly important part of the magnetism of a socialistic brand, as modern consumers use trademarks in order to communicate with each other through the commodities they consume.[91] Socialistic brands offer certain truly unique messages that convey identity, varying from endorsement of the national history, sophistication expressed through choices of vintage commodities, style evoking the bygone days or simply an identity that is rooted in past personal experiences. These messages do not have to be true to the reality of the socialis-

---

n_a_Bottle_The_Uneasy_Circulation_of_Palestinian_Olive_Oil> accessed 25.6.2016, 18.

87 Moore, (*supra* n. 3) 343.
88 Berdahl (*supra* n. 6), 199, 200.
89 Beebe "The Semiotic Account..." (*supra* n. 30), 62.
90 *Ibid.*
91 Bosland (*supra* n. 75), 13.

tic times. They can be nostalgic reproductions and falsifications of the experiences of the past[92].

To show the uniqueness of the messages that socialistic brands offer we could once again employ the example of Unitra. Since there were almost no Polish competitors in the market for audio equipment, the sign Unitra has 'a monopoly' to certain messages.

Today a person wearing a replica of Sn-50 or another Unitra product communicates through this endorsement her savvies of Polish popular audio culture. Since this message can't be communicated through consumption of other brands, exclusivity to it and with it it's cultural connotations, would give a proprietor of an unjustifiably appropriated brand a far reaching advantage over its competitors. This advantage would be gained without bringing any benefits to consumers, as today a magnetism of proportional strength would have had to been 'earned' through years of providing consumers with quality commodities.

The extent that these semiotic findings affect the situation of various undertakings will vary depending on the characteristics of a given product market and the sophistication of the end users. However, empirical evidence of advertising methods employed by Ursus, a Polish producer of agricultural equipment and machines[93], suggests that even in cases of markets characterised by specialised end users the magnetism of a socialistic brand conveys extensive value.

Semiotics offer a sound explanation of how cultural connotations of the socialistic brands can make them highly distinctive and valuable today. An abundance of unique messages and references, which are semiotically connected to these signs through their cultural connotations, contribute to their magnetism.

Signs, as with the language and the culture they belong to, cannot exist without people. This has been recognised in semiotics, which identifies the phenomenon of answerability.[94] It is through the answerability of the user that a sign gains life, shape and meaning. Recognising this, modern branding aims to create an active emotional response of consumers through use of the distinctiveness and uniqueness of socialistic brands.

---

92 Berdahl (*supra* n. 6), 202, 207.

93 See: History of Ursus on their official web page <http://en.ursus.com.pl/History> accessed 25.6.2016.

94 Mikhail Bakhtin, Vadim Liapunov (tr), Michael Holquist & Vadim Liapunov (eds) "Art and Answerability" (University of Texas Press, 1990), 2.

This is most effective through creating understanding of the brand in users' minds by referring to their memory, identity, feelings, in all of which cultural connotations play a vital part.[95] To be able to fully answer whether the unique social connotations of socialistic brands justify a call for their additional protection, we must consider how such magnetism translates to individual and group behaviour.

D. Implications of social psychology

One would be right to ask how the magnetism of a socialistic brand translates to human behaviour. Moreover, if only a marginal group of end users feels such magnetism, how does it affect the views of the majority? The 'minority influence', a phenomenon first described by Serge Moscovici[96] offers a potential answer to these questions.

Minority influence is a phenomenon of social influence attributed to an exposure of the majority to a consistent minority view. This influence is felt by the majority only after a period of time and generally leads to private acceptance or even internalisation of the views expressed.

Certain conditions have to be met in order for the minority effect to take place: consistency of the minority in their opinion, confidence that the views expressed are correct, the opinion must appear to be unbiased to the remaining part of the society and it must be resistant to the social abuse and pressure of the majority. It should be noted that Moscovici's theory has been the subject of criticism.[97] However, since it is the most established theory debunking the one-sided conceptualization of social

---

95 Mikhail Bakhtin, Vern W. McGee (tr), Caryl Emerson and Michael Holquist (eds) "Speech Genresand, Other Late Essays" (University of Texas Press, 2006), 163.

96 Serge Moscovici, Maria Zavalloni, "The Group as a Polarizer of Attitudes" (1969) 12 Journal of Personality and Social Psychology 2, 125; Serge Moscovici, Social influence and social change (Academic Press 1976); Serge Moscovici, "Toward a Theory of Conversion Behaviour" in Leonard Berkowitz (eds), *Advances in Experimental Social Psychology vol 13* (Academic Press 1980).

97 Peter Kelvin, "Book Review: Social Influence and Social Change by Serge Moscovic" (1979) 9 European Journal of Social Psychology, 441; Saul McLeod "Moscovici and Minority Influence" (*Simple Psychology*, 2007) <www.simplypsychology.org/minority-influence.html> accessed 26.5.2016.

influence[98], it seems most suited to serve as the basis of our consideration. Furthermore, results of other behaviourist experiments[99] suggest that some of the requirements indicated by Moscovici, most notably the consistency of views, might not even be prerequisite for the minority effect to take place.

Let us imagine an extreme hypothetical scenario of a fictional socialistic brand Comrade in a post-socialistic country in which a small minority of end users expresses the view 'I desire Comrade-branded sweets'. It is based solely on the magnetism of the brand. This minority is limited to some end users who remember the Comrade-branded commodities from the times of socialism. After the fall of socialism all socialistic brand have been abandoned in this hypothetical country. Currently there are no brands of sweets or any other brands on this market which evoke connections to the times of socialism. The view has been expressed by the minority consistently since the Comrade branded sweets disappeared from the market.[100]

Due to the low level of complexity of the view 'I desire Comrade-branded sweets'[101], the bar for the minority effect to take place would be set rather low. Firstly, the minority view in our case would easily meet the consistency requirement. The minority has to be consistent in its view as to the desire itself, not in the reasoning behind their craving of the Comrade-branded sweets. It is of little relevance whether the Comrade-branded sweets are desired due to such circumstances as fond memories associated with these commodities or general nostalgia for socialism, as long as the end user express the view. Secondly, the requirement of confidence in the fact that the views presented are correct would also be easily met. It would be very difficult to question correctness of consumer preferences unless

---

98 Charlan Jeanne Nemeth, „ Minority Influence Theory" in Paul A. M. Van Lange, Arie W. Kruglanski and E. Tory Higgins (eds), *Handbook of Theories in Social Psychology vol 2* (Sage 2011), 364.

99 Nemeth (*supra* n.98), 364; Charlan Jeanne Nemeth „The Differential Contributions of Majority and Minority Influence" (1986) 93 Psychological Review 1, 30.

100 The minority size would be subject to change through time. Some would abandon their views; others would revert or even re-discover the view through the experiences with the new brands or other experiences.

101 Compared to other views such as for example 'The Roman Catholic Church should accept divorces' which bring with them much more complex considerations which in turn make them in some circumstances harder to accept by the majority.

there are some additional extreme circumstances. Thirdly, the opinion would most likely appear unbiased to the majority as it would be judged as no more biased that other typical consumer preferences. Finally, the opinion must be resistant to the social abuse and pressure of the majority. Again, this view is no more biased than other consumer preferences. Furthermore, due to specific characteristics of the socialist market and the lack of alternatives, the Comrade brand would have been used often and with high intensity. This would translate to its strongly vested presence in the collective memories of the society. The brand would have been referred to in cultural media. The majority end user would be affected by these sources, thus making them receptive to the magnetism of the brand. Due to the abundance of cultural connotations, the majority would be very likely to accept the view. Only in particular strong cases, characterised by extreme historical aversion to a sign and its connotations, would the majority strongly oppose such views.[102] It should be noted that even in societies that have been widely known to perceive the socialist period negatively, socialistic brands possess strong magnetism. Mere years into unification of Germany, so many East German consumers showed such strong preference towards eastern socialistic brands that specialty shops offering them emerged.[103]

Taking all of this into the account, it is highly likely that even a socialistic brand characterised by magnetism felt only by a limited minority could gain a wide appeal through the minority influence. Even in extreme examples, there would be a strong incentive for the undertaking to obtain such socialistic brands.

Brand owners benefit from the minority effect through exposure of the majority to the minority views. This could be achieved through marketing actions but also indirectly through channels of information, such as news articles. In many instances due to the minority views concerning a given socialistic brands, news of a 're-launch' of it will be considered newsworthy.[104]

---

102 A real-life example of similar circumstances would be the Palestinian fair trade olive oil. Through circumstances of hardship in producing it, its image has become so strongly associated with the Israeli occupation that it is almost impossible for it to become free of this meaning. It has become a 'brand' of the Israeli occupation. (See. Meneley (*supra* n. 91), 18).

103 Berdahl (*supra* n. 6), 200.

104 *Supra* n. 4, 5.

An example of a successful use of such channels would be the above presented case of Pewex.

 Another example of utilisation of the minority would be the case of the audio equipment brand Unitra. Its owners have utilised a particularly interesting strategy by actively moderating a social media page that purposefully unites both the fans of the old products and the purchaser and fans of the new post-2014 products.[105]

The example of the Pan Tu Nie Stał brand could also be used. The majority of buyers of the commodities of the brand are aged 18-34[106], of which only a small proportion are likely to remember the socialist period. Pan Tu Nie Stał can serve as an example of how strongly the cultural connotations residing in signs associated with socialism translate to their magnetism, in turn allowing for the formation of strong emotional bonds in the minds of consumers through such social phenomena as minority effect.

Lastly, it should be noted that the minority effect is but one of many social phenomena that can help facilitate a more comprehensive understanding of the complexity of processes that are behind the attractiveness of a trademark. While the constraints of the format of this thesis mean that it would be impossible to name all such phenomenon, let alone present or analyse them here, it is paramount to point out that the phenomena observed by sociologists, psychologists and anthropologists show that the attractiveness of a sign is never a result of just the effort of the proprietor of the trademark. It is a result of collective use of the sign by all its users.

E. Conclusion

Socialistic brands were used as carriers of commercial connotations in highly specific historical circumstances. As a result of this, they have acquired very strong cultural connotations, which in many instances have dominated their commercial connotation. Both types of connotation are strongly intertwined, since socialistic brands originated primarily as commercial signs. Thus, neither the cultural nor the commercial connotations are likely to fully overshadow the other. The unique magnetism of these

---

105 Unitra – official facebook page <https://www.facebook.com/unitrapl> accessed 25.6.2016.
106 Author's interview with the owners of Pan Tu Nie Stał (5.9.2015.).

brands derives from both of these groups of connotations, however it is the cultural ones that make these brands so unique and shape their magnetism and thus their value. Their value should be primarily attributed not to the effort of the entities that used these brands during socialism, but rather to the peculiar type of historical circumstances that increased the prominence of signs and the memory of the society relying on the collective replay of their cultural connotations. Emotional branding is highly dependent on utilising social, psychological and cultural phenomenon, which rely on the connection between a brand and a person. In other words, cultural connotation of these signs translate to their commercial value. Therefore brand owner's interests are strongly vested in maintaining and strengthening these connotations. Furthermore, due to the strength of the cultural connotations and the fact that they were gained through commercial use, the commercial connotations are unlikely to dominate the meanings of socialistic brands. This is true even in cases in which a brand has been in continuous commercial use after the fall of the socialism and its market presence was constantly equally strong as the one in socialism.

Generally speaking, socialistic brands have been and are registered as trademarks by two types of entities, those which are in relations of succession to the earlier users of the brand from the times of socialism; and others which have no such relations. The fact that a socialistic brand was never registered or was abandoned after the fall of socialism might play a role in how such relation of succession is defined in a given case.

Taking into the account the economic justification of trademarks, it seems that in cases of clear direct succession such registrations should be allowed, as it leads to limiting the consumer search cost by showing them which company is the legal successor and provides incentives for the successors to invest in the quality of the commodities. However, there is a strong public policy interest in preventing cases of registration in which there is no clear case of succession between the registrant and the original socialist user. In these cases, there is no connection of the registrant to the commercial connotations of the sign that could justify gaining trademark exclusivity over the magnetism. Allowing for such registrations is in conflict with the need for the trademark to remain competition-neutral[107], as it

---

107 "Study on the Overall Functioning of the European Trade Mark System" (Max Planck Institute for Innovation and Competition Law Munich 2011) <http://www. ip.mpg.de/fileadmin/user_upload/mpi_final_report.pdf > accessed 25.6.2016, 52, p. 1.30.

promotes 'hijacking' abandoned socialistic brands, magnetism of which can easily be 'awoken' thus discouraging investment in quality of the products, which itself should be the main force shaping the magnetism of trademarks. Such grant of rights would be unjustifiable as they do not reward the 'labour' of the registrant but rather a savvy business decision of appropriating a sign.[108] Trademark law should not to be used as a facilitator of appropriation of signs with strong cultural connotations from the public domain. It should be used as it was intended, namely, to allow proprietors protection for the connotation they have nurtured themselves.[109]

Although cultural significance as such does not constitute an obstacle to registration, recognition of the cultural connotations of signs is not alien to the trademark doctrine. Such connotations already play a vital role in accessing many grounds of revocation and validity of the trademarks, such as descriptiveness. Furthermore, recognition of the need to limit registration of socialistic brands is in line with one of the foundations of the recent reform of EU trademark law. Namely, a call for the trademark law to more fully recognise the public and private interests affected by the acquisition of distinctive signs.[110] Since trademark law regulates use of signs it should recognise the implications that other social sciences have with regards to distinctiveness and uniqueness of signs.[111] Cultural signs are often described as belonging to society as a whole.[112] The fact that they are nurtured by an entire community, rather than a single individual or undertaking, entails that they should remain outside of the scope of trademark law.[113] There are also indications that the unencumbered com-

---

108 Katya Assaf, "The Dilution of Culture and the Law of trademarks" (2009) 49 IDEA – The intellectual Property Law Review 1 <http://ssrn.com/abstractc=1410 590> accessed 25.6.2016, 77.

109 Jennifer Davis, "Between a Sign and a Brand" in L. Bently, Jennifer Davis & J.C. Ginsburg (eds) *Trademarks and Brands* (Cambridge 2008), 82.

110 "Study on..." (*supra* n. 107), 55, p. 1.40.

111 Susy Frankel, "Trademarks and Traditional Knowledge and Cultural Intellectual Property Rights", 1 Victoria University of Wellington Legal Research Papers 6, 30, <http://papers.ssrn.com/abstract=1003608> accessed 16.6.2016.

112 Assaf (*supra* n. 107), 77.

113 Jonathan E. Schroeder, "Brand Culture: Trade Marks, Marketing and Consumption" in Jane Ginsburg, Lionel Bently & Jennifer Davis (eds) *Trade Marks and Brands An Interdisciplinary Critique* (Cambridge University Press 2008), 174.

mercial availability of cultural signs creates added value for the economy.[114]

It might be argued that since socialistic brands originated as commercial signs they should not be allowed the same treatment as the purely cultural ones. It would be a mistake to embrace such stance. In a world of rapidly advancing commoditisation of culture one is at loss to find signs with purely commercial or cultural origins or connotations. It might also be argued that socialistic brands are 'too young' to be considered as truly valuable cultural symbols, that they are purely an episodic phenomenon. In response to this we should ask ourselves this: if the current trend of belittling the impact of trademark law on culture and society continues will it be even possible for any of such 'mature' distinctive cultural symbols to emerge? Because of their magnetism they will surely be appropriated on their way to obtaining that 'mature' status. Trademark law should recognise the public policy interest in keeping signs outside of its exclusivity not only for the sake of facilitating the cultural exchange but also for the sake of preventing trademark law from warping into a field of law that facilitates behaviours contrary to its justification.

---

114 See among others: Kristofer Erickson, Paul Heald, Fabian Homberg, Martin Kretschmer and Dinusha Mendis, "Copyright and the Value of the Public Domain" (CREATe 2015) < http://www.create.ac.uk/publications/copyright-and-the-value-of-the-public-domain/> accessed 16.9.2016.

IV. Unjustifiable appropriation

A. *Introduction and scope of the consideration*

In general, unjustifiable appropriation of a socialistic brand will occur in instances in which an entity gains legally sanctioned exclusivity over such sign or a sign confusingly similar to it, without justifiable grounds. Due to the unique magnetism of these signs, instances in which a grant of exclusivity is justified should be limited to cases of clear succession of undertakings. Namely, instances in which a new post-socialist undertaking can prove that the continuity of the business goodwill of the undertaking connected to the commercial connotations of the sign justify a grant of exclusivity over it.

There are potentially many types of behaviours that may constitute an unjustifiable appropriation of these signs. Some might have occurred as early as during the process of privatisation at the outset of the market transformations of a given post-socialist country. Such behaviours should be analysed within the context of law regulating such issues as the succession of enterprises, privatisation of public assets and use of company names. This has been the case with some socialistic brands. For example, specific succession issues were raised in the case of bicycle and motorcycle brand Romet[115]. These fields of law have not been harmonised within the EU, and in many cases the relevant national acts have been amended numerous times since the initial wave of privatisation. Shedding light on this area would therefore require an in depth analysis of the particularities of numerous legal acts, which is not possible due to the format constraints of this thesis. Having this in mind, the corner stone of the considerations presented is trademark law, with further areas of law being evoked with an aim of highlighting other particular issues on the case to case basis. This area is the focus also due to the powerful implications arising from obtaining trademark exclusivity over signs with such unique and strong magnetism as socialistic brands.

---

115 Judgement of WSA in Warsaw of 7.1.2014, VI SA/Wa 1716/13.

How powerful some of the socialistic marks can become is illustrated by the example of the Prince Polo. This chocolate waffle brand is so well known on the Polish market that its proprietors were confident in evoking this mark as a ground for invalidation of the Polish national mark of the internationally known Marco Polo clothing brand.[116]

pic. 7: Prince Polo then and now.

(sources: http://41.media.tumblr.com/5ceb5a6f9f7bfd661a6ba906a39ff25b/tumblr_nb9 zp5qOIC1tf142yo1_1280.jpg; http://www.tabele-kalorii.pl/photo-003604/Wafelek-Pri nce-Polo-Classic-XXL.jpg)

The unique magnetism of socialistic brands is territorial in its character. Thus, socialistic brands should be treated differently only within post-socialist country in which the brands' magnetism would have an effect on trade[117]. Naturally, particularities of the national laws will influence the level of protection these signs can be afforded.

The core of the considerations of this paper is based on the existing provisions of law. It is centred on cases involving successors of state owned companies, which highlight legal issues related to socialistic brands. At the same time, the legal provisions analysed are evaluated in terms of their potential as obstacles against unjustifiable registrations.

B. Trademark law

1. Introduction

TMD sets forth grounds of trademark revocation and invalidation.[118] The majority of these are mandatory whilst implementation of some is voluntary.

---

116 Judgement of NSA of 12.7.2011, II GSK 746/10.
117 "Study on…" (*supra* n. 107), p. 62.
118 Art. 3, 4 TMD.

The issue of whom should have the legitimacy to raise these grounds has not been addressed in the TMD. National legislators have been given freedom in this substantive area. As a result, the following general observation might only be partially applicable to other legal systems of post-socialist countries. Until recently, in accordance to the Polish Industrial Law Act[119] (hereinafter: 'IPA'), anyone was able to submit information stating any grounds of refusal following the publication of a trademark application. This institution resembled a Roman law action of 'actio popularis' and required no legitimate interest.[120] In comparison to this, the circle of actors with legitimacy to raise grounds of invalidity was greatly limited. It was constrained to actors who were able to successfully prove their legitimate interests[121] and the President of the Patent Office of the Republic of Poland or the Prosecutor General in cases involving public interests.[122] This carried profound implications. Firstly, since the above indicated authorities were not legally obliged to act, but rather had an option of acting, there was no guarantee that they would do so, despite the fact that unlike in the majority of the trademark law systems, the Polish Patent Patent Office was until recently obliged to examine ex oficio both absolute and relative obstacles of registration. Secondly, in accordance to the Polish jurisprudence, the decisive circumstance in determining whether an actor had legitimate interest in this context was dependent on whether the trademark exclusivity in question deprived or would have deprived her of the right to use the sign.[123] This, combined with the necessity to bear the costs of legal proceedings, meant that instances in which these grounds were raised were limited to disputes between the competing entities. Thus in cases of successful registrations of abandoned socialistic brands, there were rarely any actors having interests in ensuring that a sign

---

119 Art. 143 IPA before the 15.4.2016 amendment (Ustawa z dnia 30 czerwca 2000 r. Prawo własności przemysłowej, Dz.U. 2001 nr 49 poz. 508 with changes). This act has been amended by: Ustawa z dnia 11 września 2015 r. o zmianie ustawy – Prawo własności przemysłowej, Dz.U. 14.10.2015 poz. 1615; and Ustawa z dnia 24 lipca 2015 r. o zmianie ustawy – Prawo własności przemysłowej oraz niektórych innych ustaw, Dz.U. 31.8.2015 poz. 1266, which entered into force on the 15.4.2016 and 1.12.2015 respectfully.

120 Andrzej Szewc in Ryszard Skubisz (eds.), „System Prawa Prywatnego tom 14b Prawo własności Przemysłowej" (C·H·Beck 2012) 531, p. 29.

121 Art. 164 IPA before the recent amendments.

122 Art. 167 IPA.

123 Szpakowska-Kozłowska in Skubisz (*supra* n. 120) 1166, p. 39.

would remain outside of the exclusivity conferred by trademark law. This general observation indicates that the previously available means of combating hijacking of socialistic brands were unsatisfactory. For example, under the previously applicable law, it would have been questionable whether a non-commercial cultural entity, which had interests in a socialistic brand remaining outside of the exclusivity conferred by trademark law, would have been recognised as having legitimacy to raise these grounds.

Since the submission of this thesis the applicable Polish law has been amended. Due to the fact that the amendments have entered into force very recently it is not possible to present a comprehensive assessment of their impact on the analysed substance. However, a brief outline of these changes and a short commentary seem in order. At the core of these recent revisions is the change of the role that the Patent Office has in the trademark registration process. The relative grounds of refusal and cancelation are no longer examined ex oficio. In cases of obstacles of double identity, risk of confusion and collisions with other moral or economical rights, the proprietor of a right or an earlier trademark is subject to a deadline of three months to raise the grounds of refusal, starting from the day of the publication of the trademark application.[124] The deadline in question cannot be reinstated. Another change is the inclusion of a bar from raising same grounds based on the same rights again during the action for cancellation if these were already unsuccessfully raised during the refusal proceedings.[125] Although these changes will most likely lead to shortening of the period needed for the grant of rights, they are also likely to have a negative impact on the quality of trademark rights granted. This will especially concern applications for signs of such complex relations as socialistic brands. The shortened period will most likely have some negative impact on the amount of actors filing for refusal actions. What is more, due to the usually complex factual circumstances concerning the socialistic brands, the concerned actors might be unable to produce the required evidence and will thus be unable to effectively raise the grounds of refusal. Finally, the bar from raising the grounds again might deter such actors from raising them at the stage of refusal, forcing them to opt instead for raising them as part of an action for the cancellation. In addition to the

---

124   Art. 152[17](1) IPA as amended on 15.4.2016.
125   Art. 165(1)4) IPA as amended on 15.4.2016.

above outlined changes, Polish legislator has also decided to drop the requirement to show legal interest in order to raise the grounds of cancellation.[126] This is a much welcomed change that makes it possible for a broader group of actors to challenge decisions in instances of unjustifiable appropriations of socialistic brands. This could for example include the above mentioned non-commercial cultural entities.

2. Socialistic brands as generic terms

In order to become a trademark, a sign needs to have the capacity to distinguish a given type of commodities of one enterprise from another.[127]

An unjustifiable appropriation of a socialistic brand will take place in instances in which such brand is a subject to a trademark right, even though it has become synonymous with a given type of commodity. Unless a significant proportion of the relevant public perceives a given socialistic brand as being capable of indicating a specific commercial origin[128], these signs should be considered devoid of distinctiveness in the meaning of classical trademark doctrine, which in turn means that they should not be eligible for trademark protection.[129] Distinctiveness is assessed through the analysis of the sign as a whole.[130] Since descriptive signs may be freely used as part of complex or graphic marks[131] and since the majority of socialistic brands comprise of much more than mere words or phrases, many of them could not become generic even if phrases that form part of them have.

Thus, instances of 'hijacking' abandoned socialistic brands in which this ground could be evoked are highly limited.

The extensive use of socialistic brands during the times of socialism and their strong cultural presence today translates to a high likelihood that even fanciful word marks, such as these evoked below, could become generic.

---

126 Art. 164 as ammended on 15.4.2016.
127 Art. 3 TMD.
128 Case C-108/05 *Bovemij Verzekeringen v. Benelux-Merkenbureau* EU:C: 2006:530, ECR 2006 I-07605, p 28.
129 Art. 4 1(b) TMD.
130 *SAT. 1* (*supra* n. 19), p. 35.
131 Case C-109/97 *Windsurfing Chiemsee* EU:C:1999:230, [1999] ECR I-2779, p. 25.

Krupnik is an example of a name of a product, which has become generic primarily through its extensive use as a socialistic brand even though it predates socialism in Poland. This old Polish term originally used to designate a person who manufactures or sells grits (also a traditional Polish soup) has been used as a brand of alcoholic drink by many entitles belonging to the state combine Polmos. Based on evidence which included entries from dictionaries published as early as 1966, the Supreme Administrative Court approved the decision of the Patent Office and decided that the name 'krupnik' was a generic name for an alcoholic drink based on honey and spices, both at the time of application by one of the successors of the combine in 1993 and at the time of issuing the judgement in 2015.[132]

However, it should be kept in mind that the distinctiveness of a sign may be re-acquired through various attempts that lead to re-establishing the associations of a sign with an undertaking.[133] Poland has chosen to implement a non-obligatory TMD provision in accordance to which grounds for revocation or invalidity due to lack of distinctiveness cannot be raised if the distinctive character was acquired after the date of application.[134] This makes evoking this ground even more difficult.

An example of how complex and difficult assessments of distinctiveness could be in cases of socialistic brand is that of the chocolate candy brand Ptasie Mleczko (literally 'bird's milk', an old Polish idiom for an 'unobtainable delicacy'). For the last nine years this word mark has been a subject of legal battles, at the centre of which lies the issue of its generic status.[135] The word trademark currently belongs to a successor of the original producers of the chocolate candy. As in other cases of socialistic brands, the history of the brand is full of turmoil. The company Wedel (named after the family name of the founder) was founded in 1851[136] and the term Ptasie Mleczko was registered as a trademarked before the Second World War. The undertaking was later nationalised, which in turn led

---

132 Judgment of NSA of 14.1.2015, II GSK 1815/14.

133 *Chiemsee* (*supra* n. 131), p. 45-46.

134 Art. 3 (3) TMD.

135 Mikołaj Lech, „Po 58 Latach Wedel Odzyskuje Prawo do Nazwy "PTASIE MLECZKO"'" (*Wyborcza biz*, 10.11.2014) <http://wyborcza.biz/Prawo/1,128894, 16946756,Po_58_latach_Wedel_odzyskuje_prawo_do_nazwy__PTASIE.html> accessed 25.6.2016.

136 Official Wedel page <https://www.wedelpijalnie.pl/pl/o-nas/e-wede> accessed 25.6.2016.

to the abandonment of the Ptasie Mleczko trademark in 1956. During the socialist period the name Wedel was used not as a primary brand but rather as a sub-brand of products including 'ptasie mleczko'. The phrase Ptasie Mleczko has been re-registered in 2006.[137] It seems that at least in some periods the phrase was used in a generic way, particularly when these types of products were produced by many entities within a socialist production combine. The term has been used differently throughout its history, both as word mark and figurative mark. Competing companies have been offering and still offer 'ptasie mleczko' chocolate. Finally, many of the contemporary efforts of the current proprietor are clearly aimed at combating generic use of the brand name, including sending cease and desist letters to bloggers who use the term 'ptasie mleczko' without mentioning Wedel in recipe articles[138]. Naturally, all these changing circumstances should be taken into the account in determining how the relevant public perceives this phrase[139], which as this case shows, might make such assessments particularly cumbersome. One should conclude that due to a complicated history of the socialistic brands, assessment of their distinctiveness may be extremely difficult.

pic. 8: Ptasie Mleczko then and now.

(sources: http://retro.pewex.pl//uimages/services/pewex/i18n/pl_PL/201211/13528217 70_by_Sebastian_500.jpg; http://bi.gazeta.pl/im/16/7a/ca/z13269526Q,Jeszcze-kilka-l at-temu-pudelko-wedlowskiego-przysm.jpg)

---

137 National no. of the right 266762.
138 Artur Kawik, „Walka o „Ptasie Mleczko®" Przyczyną Kryzysu Wizerunkowego Wedla" (*Socialpress* 13.2.2012) < http://socialpress.pl/2012/02/walka-o-ptasie-ml eczko-przyczyna-kryzysu-wizerunkowego-wedla/> accessed 25.06.201^.
139 *Chiemsee* (*supra* n. 131), p. 39.

3. Socialistic brands as indicators of characteristics of commodities

An unjustifiable appropriation of a socialistic brand will occur in instances in which it has become a subject of a trademark right, although it has become synonymous with certain characteristics of a given commodity.[140] This ground of refusal or invalidity is narrower than genericism as the sign is descriptive only with regards to certain types of goods or services.[141] It is enough if such sign points only to one of the characteristics of a given commodity.[142] It is also sufficient if it is reasonable to assume that such an association may be established in the future.[143] The applicability of this provision is limited to signs that may serve to designate, either directly or by reference, one of the essential characteristics of commodities in normal usage.[144] This greatly limits the application of these grounds to the socialistic brands as it leaves out of its scope instances in which the brand evokes connections to a country's history, culture or any other non-direct characteristics. As in the case of genericism, a sign which consist of more elements (a figurative mark for example) will not be automatically excluded from the registration as other parts of the sign might be distinctive.[145] In the cases of various versions of figurative marks with phrase 'Lublin Spirytus Rektyfikowany' ('rectified alcohol of Lublin', Lublin is a capital city of an eastern region of Poland), even though this phrase itself was descriptive, the signs which were in fact updated forms of a socialistic brands were declared distinctive as a whole.[146]

This ground was also raised is the case of the socialistic brand Delicje (which means 'delicacies' in Polish).[147] The Delicje Szampańskie-branded jaffa cakes were first produced in the 1976 by one of the grouped units. This unit was privatised and bought by an entity that later applied for

---

140 Art. 3(1)(c) TMD.
141 Case C-265/00 *Campina Melkunie BV v Benelux* EU:C:2004:87, [2004] ECR I-01699, p. 19.
142 *Chimsee* (*supra* n. 131), p. 25; Cases c-53/01 and c-55/01 *Linde and others*, EU:C:2003:206, [2003] ECR I-03161 p. 73.
143 *Chimsee* (*supra* n. 131); T-304/06 *Reber v OHMI* [2008] EU:T:2008:268, [2008] ECR II-01927, p. 89.
144 Case C-383/99 P *Procter & Gamble* EU:C:2001:461, [2001] ECR I-06251, p. 39.
145 Szczepanowska-Kozłowska (*supra* n. 123), 587, 49.
146 Jusgements of WSA in Warsaw: of 5.9.2014, VI SA/Wa 1995/13; of 29.5.2014 VI SA/Wa 1996/13; of 29.5.2014 VI SA/Wa 1980/13.
147 Judgement of WSA in Warsaw of 21.3.2012, VI SA/Wa 1761/06.

a word mark. The complainant in this case argued that the word Delicje is a generic name for a type of a jaffa cakes. She argued that until the registration of the word mark Delicje in 1991[148], the brand for this pastry products were in fact Delicje Szampańskie. The court assessed that due to the time of registration the previous trademark act should apply. This meant that the ground of descriptiveness could be raised five years after the grant of the right only if the applicant was acting in bad faith. Despite the fact that the claimant failed to prove the bad faith of the registrant, the court analysed the submitted evidence, which included: a legal and linguistic opinions, an article from a 1983 pastry magazine, a socialism-era industry standard and an entry from a cooking book; and concluded that these would be not enough to prove descriptiveness. This Delicje case also shows that in many instances intertemporal legal provision might mandate application of particular norms from previous legal acts that can further complicate cases involving socialistic brands.

pic. 9:   Package of Delicje Szampańskie from 1976 and Delicje from 2015.

(sources: http://designofprl.tumblr.com/image/90461746413; http://www.darpolpolskis klep.com/1834-1854 thickbox/wedel-delicje-szampaskie-pomaraczowe-294g.jpg)

4. Bad faith registration

In accordance to TMD bad faith is a non-mandatory and independent[149] ground of revocation and invalidity[150]. The concept of bad faith is as an

---

148   National no. of the right: 070513.
149   Alexander Tsoutsanis, "Trade Mark Registration in Bad Faith" (Oxford 2010) 338, p. 20.94.
150   Art. 4 (4)(g) TMD.

autonomous concept of European Union law and thus should be interpreted identically on the entirety of the territory of the community.[151] However, due to the complex nature and character of this concept, which could perhaps be described as a 'backdoor' through which other systems of norms can be brought into trademark law, uncertainties with regard to how it should be construed prevail[152].

The acknowledgment of the autonomous character of the concept of bad faith seems to confirm that it has its own meaning and is not synonymous with concepts of bad faith from other branches of law, including that from civil law. In fact, the concept of bad faith in trademark is interpreted in Polish law as a narrower one than her civil law counterpart.[153] Instances of registration in bad faith should not be equated with theses envisaged in other grounds of revocation and invalidation.[154] For example, an instance in which registrant knew that a sign applied for was generic, could not be considered a registration in bad faith. The bad faith in trademark law seems to be focused on the manner in which the registration has been made and its potential impact.[155]

In general, registration in bad faith takes place when an applicant files for registration knowing, or if circumstances show that he should have known, that his actions are against accepted principles of ethical behaviour or honest commercial practices and that they are aimed at gaining an undue advantage. This means that this ground is potentially applicable in cases of registrations of both signs similar to and identical with socialistic brands.

Since in majority of cases trademarks are being registered by legal persons, a question should be raised regarding the manner of assessing their behaviour. In accordance to the theory established in the Polish civil

---

151 *Malaysia Diary* (*supra* n. 19), p. 29.
152 Tsoutsanis (*supra* n. 149), 92.
153 This interpretation of bad faith on the grounds of trademark law as an autonomous concept is in conformity with the prevailing opinions on the grounds of other legal systems, including German. (*See*: Tsoutsanis (*supra* n. 149), 187 – 188, p. 7.05 – 7.06).
154 Ewa Nowińska, Michał du Vall „Pojęcie Złej Wiary w Prawie Znaków Towarowych" in *Księga pamiątkowa z okazji 85-lecia Ochrony Własności Przemysłowej w Polsce* (Urząd Patentowy RP, 2003), 145.
155 Ryszard Skubisz, „Zgłoszenie Znaku Towarowego w Złej Wierze" in L. Ogiegło, W. Popiołek, M. Szpunar (red.) *Rozprawy prawnicze, Księga pamiątkowa Profesora Maksymiliana Pazdana* (Zakamycze 2005), 1342.

law[156], since such entities act through their bodies, the key for determining bad faith is the awareness and behaviour of the members of such bodies. In many cases this proves problematic as decision making processes in enterprises often involve many such bodies. Moreover, this assessment might constitute an impenetrable maze in cases of socialistic brands, as the relevant undertakings and their bodies were subject to numerous transformations.

Neither the EUTM and TMD nor the corresponding Polish legal provisions contain a definition of bad faith. The lawmaker has purposefully regulated this substance in a general way to allow for a flexible interpretation of this term.[157] In assessing bad faith the subjective circumstances of a given case should be judged through reference to objective circumstances.[158] All the circumstances relevant to the case which pertained at the time of filing of the application should be taken into the account.[159]

A case concerning a figurative mark Sks Start Łódź Rok Założenia 1953 (Sports Club Start Łódź, year of est. 1953) did not concern a per se socialistic brand, as it involved an attempt to re-register a name of a sports club. However, it highlights a rich set of circumstances the types of which are likely to occur in instances of bad faith registrations of socialistic brands. In this case concerning an attempt to register a figurative mark identical to the mark which expired as a result of a failure to pay renewal fees, the court aptly pointed out a number of circumstances, which when taken together indicated that the applicant acted in bad faith.

Firstly, the sign included the phrase 'established in 1953', which in court's opinion would mean that, if the applicant was allowed to register she would benefit from suggestions to consumers that her sports club was established that year and that she is the successor of the earlier owner of the sign, when in fact the applicants club was founded only in 2005. Circumstances in which parts of the sign or the entire sign carry strong historical suggestions of the brand's long existence are likely to suggest to the end user that the proprietor is in fact the successor of the brand. How-

---

156 Judgements of the Supreme Court: of 24.10.1972, I CR 177/72, (OSNCP 10/73, p. 171); of 12.10.2007, V CSK 249/07 (OSG 2009, 4, 25).
157 Case C-529/07 *Chocoladenfabriken Lindt & Sprüngli* EU:C:2009:361, [2009] EGC I-04893, p. 74 – 75.
158 Tsoutsanis (*supra* n. 149), 131; *Chocoladenfabriken Lindt* (*supra* n. 157), p. 42.
159 *Malaysia Dairy* (*supra* n. 19), p 36; *Chocoladenfabriken Lindt* (*supra* n. 157), p. 42.

ever, as it was described, in cases of socialistic brand it is questionable if the confusion with regard of continuity of enterprises occur in all instances.

Secondly, the court observed that the applicant attempted to hijack the positive associations the brand evoked in the minds of the end users, which were a result of many years of use by another entity. This particular sports club was neither widely known in Poland, nor particularly successful. Yet the court clearly identified that the sign carried with it positive connotations in the minds of end users. This could serve as an indicator that the degree of magnetism of a sign might constitute an important factor in cases of bad faith even if it is not rooted in the quality of the commodities affixed with it.

Thirdly, the applicant admitted knowing that the mark was used to designate identical services and that the right lapsed due to unpaid fees. This shows that any factor proving the knowledge of the applicant with regard to the brand, its meaning and its current situation, might have significance in the assessment of her behaviour. With regard to the knowledge of the applicant, the CJEU also made a crucial observation that the longer an earlier mark is used the greater the likelihood that the applicant had knowledge of this earlier sign when filing for its registration.[160] It would thus be difficult to successfully argue that an applicant did not know of the socialistic brand if she filed for a similar or identical mark. However, a mere fact that the applicant possesses the knowledge of the use of the conflicting sign is itself insufficient to prove that she was in bad faith.[161]

Fourthly, the applicant previously attempted to gain exclusivity over the sign by registering an internet domain name identical to the phonetic layer of the sign. An earlier ruling issued by another court prohibited the applicant from using the name in this manner. Previous questionable conduct of the applicant should not be irrelevant when assessing whether the registration was done in bad faith.[162] Circumstances which occurred after the reg-

---

160 *Chocoladenfabriken Lindt* (*supra* n. 157), p. 39.
161 *Malaysia* (*supra* n. 19), p. 37.
162 An example of another such circumstance might be the applicant being part of the decision making bodies of the entity which used the brand before the bad faith attempt to register it (*see* Judgment of NSA of 24.5.2007, II GSK 377/06).

istration might also be vital in accessing the applicant's behaviour at the time of filing of the application.[163]

In a way of summary, since the fact patterns of the disputes regarding socialistic brands are particularly complex it is vital to recognise that many varied circumstances are relevant in investigating bad faith.

In the case of Delicje branded jaffa cookies[164] highlighted above, the complainant submitted that the applicant was in bad faith, as at the time of registration she must have known that the word Delicje is a generic term for a type of pastries. The complainant argued that the applicant sought to unfairly appropriate the sign since she knew that other producers used the phrase.[165] As proof of this, an extensive set of evidence was submitted. The court observed that the applicant was a successor of an undertaking which in 1974 was the first one among the collective to offer cookies under this name and assessed the evidence as inadequate to prove that other entities used the name 'delicje' at the time of the registration. This case shows how difficult and uncertain it is to argue that the applicant acted in bad faith, even in cases with a comprehensive set of evidence. The court would have perhaps reached a different verdict had the complainant produced direct evidence showing that other entities offered 'delicje' cookies at the time of the registration. The particularities of the time period should be kept in mind. For example, it is possible that the turmoil of restructuring and privatisation that took place in the 1990s were the main reason why the applicant was the sole producer of branded cookies at the time of the registration.

Because trademark application in bad faith is an activity consisting of unjustifiable appropriation of a mark, it is naturally necessary to prove that signs are identical, or at least similar to such a degree that it is likely to mislead the public.[166] In the case of application for a figurative sign Hortino[167], the applicant purchased one of the manufacturing units of a previously state owned frozen foods and fruit juices producer: Hortex. Hortex was a successor of the state owned company that used this brand since 1958 and possessed many corresponding trademarks, the earliest

---

163 Judgement of WSA in Warszawie of 18.1.2012 r, VI SA/Wa 1850/11; Judgement of NSA of 25.11.2009, II GSK 203/09.
164 See page 49.
165 Judgement of WSA in Warsaw of 21.3.2012, VI SA/Wa 1761/06.
166 Judgements of NSA: of 25.5.2006, II GSK 66/06; of 8.1.2014, II GSK 1542/12.
167 Judgement of NSA of 24.5.2005, II GSK 63/05.

from 1961[168]. After taking over the unit the applicant informed the clients of the unit that she would start operating under the sign Hortino and extended a business offer to them. Afterwards she applied to register a figurative mark Hortino. The court decided that the applicant acted in bad faith, pointing out that the Hortex brand existed on the market for many years, which increased the possibility of consumers confusing it with a similarly looking and sounding Hortino. Yet again, this signals that the historical pedigree of socialistic brands and its effect on the signs' magnetism is not lost to the courts. However, it might be questioned if the court would have ruled similarly had there been no goodwill attached to Hortex.

Another socialistic brand case concerned a word and figurative mark CNOS (abbreviation of the phrase 'company of horticultural seeds and nursery') which was used by actors grouped under a single entity.[169] After the division, none of the newly established undertakings, including the applicant, gained exclusive rights to the brand. The court derived from this that all of the enterprises created from the group were entitled to use the shortcut CNOS as part of their names. The court rightfully concluded that applicant's actions were aimed at unjustifiable appropriation of the brand. As an entity that used to belong to the collective, she must have been aware of the implications of her actions. However, it is rather puzzling that the court so effortlessly accepted that different competing entities are using the same or confusingly similar signs for indicating the source of the same type of commodities.

Herbapol The case concerning an application for the trademark Herbapol Wrocław[170], similarly to the previous case, highlights an issue of multiple successors of a socialistic enterprise operating under confusingly similar trademarks. The complainant was an administrator of the collective trademark. She pointed out that at the date of filing of the application, the applicant was among the group of undertakings entitled to use the collective mark which differs from the applied mark only in the lack of inclusion of the geographical name of the city of Wrocław (one of the main cities of Poland). Therefore, the applicant must have known that her behaviour was unfair. The court did not access bad

---

168 National no. of the right: 43037.
169 Judgement of NSA of 4.6.2002, II SA 3867/01.
170 Judgement of WSA in Warsaw of 14.6.2013, VI Sa/Wa 101/13; Judgement of NSA of 9.1.2015 II GSK 2062/13.

faith in this case, as it rightly held that the application should be revoked on the grounds of it being confusingly similar to the collective mark. However, similar circumstances might help in assessing bad faith in other cases.

In many cases entities using the same socialistic brands had been coexisting for a substantial time before the application for a trademark was filed. It might be thus inquired how previous conduct of tolerating such use affects the assessment of bad faith. In this regard, a Dutch Supreme Court ruling in the subject of Russian socialistic brands Moskovskaya, Na Zdorovye and Stolichnaya should be evoked. The court ruled that tolerating use of a brand as such does not constitute a valid defence against claims of bad faith registration. A defence would be available only if an explicit consent has been given by the right holder and the applicant was aware of this at the time of the application[171]. This view seems to find approval in a ruling of the Polish Supreme Court in the substance of the right to use a business name.[172]

In the way of summary, bad faith is in particular dependent on three types of factors: whether the application was characterised by the intent to prevent others from using that sign, what degree of the protection of the legal sign is involved and applicants' knowledge of the use of the similar of identical sign for the similar or identical commodities.[173] Bad faith is an elusive ground of revocation and proving it in cases of socialistic brands is highly difficult and often requires producing evidence that is difficult to obtain. Case law shows that even in the same jurisdiction and in similar fact patterns, two courts are likely to decide differently. However, due to its flexibility and numerous case law, bad faith is perhaps the most versatile obstacle against registration of signs in cases in which commercial interests of third parties are not directly involved[174]. These cases could be interpreted as instances in which cultural signs are appropriated in order to extract money from other entities engaging in cultural activity to prohibit them from use of such signs. Such interpretation would broaden the group of actors with legitimacy to oppose such registrations. CJEU refers to 'nature' and 'degree of legal protection'[175] of the mark as circumstances

---

171 Judgement of the Dutch Supreme Court of 20.12.2013, 12/05013 TT/AS.

172 Judgement of the Supreme Court of 14.2.2003, IV CKN 1782/00.

173 Tsoutsanis, (*supra* n. 149), 341, p. 20.99.

174 "Study on…" (*supra* n. 107), 154, p. 3.122.

175 *Chocoladenfabriken Lindt* (*supra* n. 157), 53.

that should be taken into account. This may allow for evoking such characteristics of socialistic brands as their cultural connotations. However, it could be noted that in many instances, just as in the two bad faith cases decided by the CJEU, at the centre lies a sign used by other entities than the registrant. As it was shown in the Delicje case, in the 'abandonment' scenarios, it may be questionable whether a sign is being used in a trademark sense by any entities, be it commercial or cultural. This in turn makes it possible to argue that there is no obstacle to registration and that at least from the bad faith point of view, such signs should be free to be remonopolised.

5. Contrary to public policy

As it has been pointed out in the section III of this thesis, acts of misappropriation of socialistic brands' magnetism should be considered as contrary to public policy. Groups of signs that can be revoked on this ground are not limited to signs that are themselves contrary to the public policy. It also includes signs, the use of which and the consequences of it, would be contrary to the public policy.[176] Unfortunately, the CJEU case law does not explicitly recognise the particular public interest that would be needed in cases of socialistic brands.[177] However, since each of the absolute grounds for refusal are reflecting different considerations, the type of the public policy they embody is also different[178]. This means that in cases of abandoned socialistic brands there is a possibility to argue that although they are primarily distinctive and unencumbered, they are cultural signs and because of this they should be kept free for everyone to use, in order to keep the trademark law competition-neutral. As in cases of other types of signs characterised by strong and unique cultural connotations it is simply contrary to apply 'first in, first served' principle to them[179]. Such an interpretation would be particularly welcome, as unlike bad faith, public policy grounds could be evoked in instances of socialistic brands being registered for other commodities than the ones they were originally used for.

---

176 Szczepanowska-Kozłowska (*supra* n. 123) 605, 96.
177 "Study on…" (*supra* n. 107), 56, p. 1.41.
178 *SAT. 1* (*supra* n. 19) p. 25.
179 Frankel (*supra* n. 111) p. 32.

6. Other grounds of refusal

There are other grounds of refusal that might be raised in order to challenge attempts to register socialistic brands as trademarks. Among them are the ones which seem particularly connected to the nature of the magnetism of the socialistic brands, namely grounds concerning signs having symbolic value and signs deceiving the public.

Poland has chosen to introduce a non-mandatory ground of refusal and invalidity of signs of high symbolic value. Polish commentators identify these symbols as evoking feelings of honour, pride, national tradition or authority of the state.[180] Since the times of socialism are a highly debated political and historical issue, companies offering commodities using socialistic brands tend to distance themselves from socialism itself.[181] Even though socialistic brands might have a specific magnetism that is derived from almost 50 years of historical use in peculiar circumstances, it would be highly contested to elevate socialistic brands to the category of symbols of high symbolic value. In sum, it is unlikely that raising these grounds would be realistically possible in cases of registration of socialistic brands.

It is also doubtful whether it would be possible to successfully argue that re-registration of socialistic brands is deceiving the public. In the light of the CJEU interpretation, this provision applies only to cases in which a sign in its content layer includes deceiving information concerning the characteristics of the commodity[182], which is rarely the case with socialistic brands.

C. Unfair competition law

Unfair competition is widely acknowledged as a potential alternative mean of governing the use of signs in trade.[183] This area of law could be

---

180 Janusz Barta, „Przeszkody Udzielenia Prawa Ochronnego na Znak Towarowy" in Janusz Barta, Ryszard Markiewicz, Andrzej Matlak (eds) *Prawo Mediów* (Lexis-Nexis 2008), LEX no. 52747.

181 *Supra* n. 106.

182 Case C-259/04 *Emanuel* EU:C:2006:215, [2006] ECR I-03089, p 45-49. *See* also Szczepanowska-Kozłowska (*supra* n. 123) 610, p. 107-108.

183 *Inter alia see*: p. (7) TMD.

employed against torts of causing confusion and misleading the public through use of socialistic brands, misappropriation of them or any other behaviour that would fall under a general type of unfair conducts against competition. However, in the EU only selected areas of unfair completion law have been harmonised. Therefore, this area of law may very likely play a prominent role only in countries which, just as Poland, have a comprehensive set of provisions dedicated to torts of unfair conduct. In Poland this legal alternative is burdened by a narrow way in which the Polish Unfair Competition Act[184] (hereinafter: 'UCA') defines actors who have legitimacy to evoke these grounds, namely competitors and competition authorities.

The above-mentioned Hortex case is an example of a dispute concerning a socialistic brand decided on the grounds of unfair competition law. The Polish Supreme Court[185] issued a ruling in line with a previous decision of the administrative court decided on the basis of trademark law. The actions of Hortino Wrocław were characterised by bad faith and were aimed at misleading the public with regard to the origin of the products. The case of Delicje jaffa cakes was also subject to litigation on the grounds of tort of misleading the public and imitating a product.[186] Both of these cases show that unfair competition law can be used in a manner auxiliary and complementary to trademark law. Perhaps most importantly, unfair competition law could be employed to scrutinise use of the socialistic brands in cases in which more than one company is in position that justifies exclusivity over the same socialistic brand.

Herbapol Previously discussed cases of Herbapol and the CNOS reveal fallacies of the present attempts of facilitating use of the same or confusingly similar socialistic brands by many entities within one market.

The CNOS model prohibiting any singular entity from obtaining a trademark based on tolerating the use of the same sign by competing undertakings is deeply flawed[187]. Even if in such cases use of the signs would be contained to company names, the fact that these names are affixed on products means that they function as indicators of origins, in

---

184 Art. 18 UCA (Ustawa z dnia 16 kwietnia 1993 r. o zwalczaniu nieuczciwej konkurencji, Dz.U.2003.153.1503 (unified version) with changes).
185 Judgement of the Polish Supreme Court of 10.8.2006, V CSK 237/06.
186 Judgement of the Court of Appeals in Warsaw of 6.11.2015 I ACz 1640/12.
187 *Supra* n. 169.

other words as trademarks.[188] Moreover, legal uncertainty created by such state entails unnecessary legal costs for both the parties and the court system. It also leads to consumer confusion and decreases incentives to invest.

The collective sign model from the Herbapol case is also deeply flawed. Here companies founded an association, which governs the use of the collective trademark. Firstly, the way in which this collective trademarks is used, namely by encompassing the dominant figurative collective trademark in the signs used in business, does not limit search costs and in fact expands them. This fact is not mitigated by the inclusion of geographical names of the original unit of the socialist-era Herbapol, as the court pointed out in the Herbapol trademark case.[189] Secondly, consumers faced with a geographical name may very well assume that it only indicates the location of the factory from the times of socialism and conclude that all offered commodities come from the same undertaking. In instances of multiple clear succession, competing undertakings should be allowed to use such collective socialistic brand trademarks only in a manner that does not cause confusion as to the source of the commodity. Thirdly, use of socialistic brands as collective marks greatly decreases the incentive to invest in the quality of the commodities. An entitled actor will benefit from action of her competitors aimed at promoting the brand. Lastly, consequent litigation in the Herbapol Wrocław case proves that this solution does not effectively eliminate potential disputes.

The Polish legislator has recognised the need to determine which entity in entitled to the brand in multiple 'succession scenarios'.[190] Art. 7 of the UCA stipulates that in a cases of disputes arising as a result of liquidation, division or transformation of an undertaking, if the question arises as to which of the entrepreneurs is entitled to use the designation of the previous undertaking, such designation should be defined in such manner as to prevent third parties from being misled. Among the factors that should be taken into the account are both interests of the parties and other circumstances of a case, including interests of the third parties. This provision shows that there are legal means of determining which entity or entities should be entitled to a socialistic brand. Limiting the possibility of gaining

---

188   Case C-17/06 *Celine* EU:C:2007:497, [2007] EGC I-07041, p. 21 – 22.
189   *Supra* n. 167.
190   Marian Kępiński in Janusz Szwaja (red.) „Ustawa o Zwalczaniu Nieuczciwej Konkurencji Komentarz" (3rd ed. C.H.Beck 2013), 324.

exclusivity over socialistic brands would bring life to this rarely utilised provision. Especially since commentators consider it as a failed one, pointing at the abundance of post-transformation cases concerning the rights to brands decided without its use.[191] A legal landscape in which this provision would be evoked more often would likely motivate undertakings, in cases akin to Herbapol, to re-think their business strategies. Entities like Herbapol could perhaps consider embracing new, distinctive names through rebranding, whilst continuing using the collective Herbapol mark in a manner that indicates that they are successors of that company. This would allow them to benefit from the cultural connotations of this brand in a justifiable manner. Otherwise, they would have to reckon with a risk of facing an unfair completion claim.

D. Copyright Law

It might be also possible to evoke copyright law in order to prevent unfair appropriations of socialistic brands.[192] However, it may be particularly cumbersome to find a person or an entity having rights to the underlying work and thus legitimacy to raise this ground. This is due to the time that passed since a graphical design work was created and the lack of legal culture during socialism, which often led to parties paying little heed to contracting.

E. Geographical indicators

Socialistic brands might also be protected as geographical indicators. However, this model of protection is highly unsuitable for majority of socialistic brands. Its utility would be limited to cases in which many undertakings are clear successors of a socialistic entity. A high level of cooperation between the competing entities would also be required. What is more, the possibility of obtaining protection through various geographical indicator systems is usually limited to foodstuffs, which are at least in certain degree connected to a given territory. Socialistic brand products are rarely connected to territorial characteristics. Furthermore,

---

191 *Ibid.*
192 Art. 4 (4) (c) (iii) TMD.

they were and are used for other types of commodities than food products. Finally, the rationale of awarding protection to geographical indicators is rooted in preserving the quality of the products. As it has been indicated here before, the quality of commodities was not among the main factors shaping the magnetism of these brands.

F. Sui generis protection

A potential alternative solution is protecting socialistic brands on the ground of sui generis protection. This solution is by no means alien to the Polish legislator. A similar means has been employed in order to control a different set of signs with high cultural magnetism, namely: the name, likeness and the legacy of the famous Polish pianist Fryderyk Chopin.[193] A similar sui generis attempt to curb appropriation of certain vital signs was employed by the World Health Organisation with regards to non-proprietary names for pharmaceutical substances (INNs)[194].

In the case of socialistic brands, this legal mean could perhaps take form of a moderated list of signs. These signs could be registered as trademarks only in exceptional circumstances, after obtaining permission from an appropriate body. However, this solution has many flaws. Due to complex historical and cultural context of socialistic brands, such list would be much harder to compile and administer than the INNs list. This would put its reliability into question. Furthermore, introducing means limiting the possibility to use trademarks already obtained by various actors, would likely be met with a strong opposition on many legal fronts.[195] Since both trademark rights and applications have been recognised as a fundamental right by the European Court of Human Rights[196] and are considered

---

193 Michał Kruk, "Protection of Chopin's Heritage as a Sui Generis Regulation" (2010), 5 Journal of Intellectual Property Law & Practice 8, 608.

194 Senftleben, "Trademark law"(*supra* n. 41), 8.

195 Inter alia: Henning Grosse Ruse – Khan, "Protecting Intellectual Property Under BITs, FTAs and TRIPs: Conflicting Regimes or Mutual Coherence?" in C Brown, K Miles (Eds.), *Evolution in Investment Treaty Law and Arbitration*, (Cambridge University Press 2011).

196 *Anheuser-Busch Inc v Portugal, Merits*, App no 73049/01, (2007) 44 EHRR 42, IHRL 3436 (ECHR 2007). However, unlike what some of the commentators seem to be suggesting, not every measure that leads to stripping of the IP right would be precluded under the norms governing human right, as a case-by-case

investments under international investment treaties[197], implementation of this solution would likely encumber governments in international litigation. What is more, one could envisage it being labelled as nationalisation or collectivisation of trademarks, which would very likely make it an even more unpopular political choice in the post-socialist countries. Lastly, the legal history of IP protection proves that creating a new branch of IP in order to solve an inadequacy on an existing branch is never an effective solution.

---

careful balancing of all the fundamental rights concerned is required (see. B. Goebel, "Trademarks as fundamental rights – Europe",99 Trademark Reporter 2009, 951-952.).

197 B. Mercurio, "Awakening the Sleeping Giant: Intellectual Property Right in International Investment Agreement" (2012) 15 J Int Economic Law 3, 874.

V. The socialistic brands dilemma

As it has been shown in this thesis, the current legislation might at best provide an uncertain patchwork-like solution for addressing the appropriation of the socialistic brands. This is mainly due to the fact that trademark law was not designed having in mind its implications for the public domain[198], the ever intensified use of trademarks or their changing nature. Before we summarise, there are two policy suggestions that should be made.

Firstly, in cases of systems in which trademark applications are substantially examined ex officio, the easiest solution would be to amend the guidelines for trademark examiners, by including the category of socialistic brands and other signs with strong cultural connotations with explanation of the rationale behind curbing their registrations.

Secondly, national legislators should also fully recognise the profound and complex role trademarks play in influencing end user decisions and allow for a wider group of actors to have legitimacy to raise grounds of invalidity of trademark. One potential solution could involve competition authorities. They could be obliged to monitor registration of such signs and raise such grounds whenever it is justified. This competence could easily fit into the role of these watchdogs of anticompetitive behaviour, as obtaining unjustifiable exclusivity over such signs results in gaining unfair advantage over competitors[199]. As limiting the caseload of trademark offices and courts is probably among the main reasons for limiting the group of actors who have the legitimacy to lever registrations, competition authorities would also serve as a sieve. The amount of cases could be limited and the quality of the legal arguments raised would likely improve if a procedure obliging authorities to access complaints submitted by the public would be established.

---

198 Senftleben, "Trademark law…" (*supra* n. 41), 2.
199 In Poland the Office of Competition and Consumer Protection has been involved in certain disputes regarding the signs used in commerce. This includes the above addressed case of the dispute between Hortex and Hortino in which the office issued an interpretation in response to a request of a member of the parliament.

By way of summary, if both the Polish Patent Office and the courts would recognise the need to treat socialistic brands differently on the grounds of the existing law, only 'succession scenario' socialistic brands should be allowed to remain subject to trademark exclusivity. Attempts to unjustifiably appropriate socialistic brands in cases in which these have become generic or descriptive would be addressed as any other signs. Cases in which abandoned socialistic brands or signs confusingly similar to them are distinctive would have to be addressed either on the grounds of bad faith registration, in cases in which they are registered and used for the same or similar commodities, or on the grounds of being contrary to public policy, in cases of registration for different commodities. The issues of scenarios in which multiple entities are justified to claim exclusivity over a socialistic brand could be addressed on the grounds of unfair competition law.

Before we pronounce this interpretation scenario as a ray of sunshine in this otherwise gloomy panorama, we should keep in mind that results of raising all of the grounds and torts mentioned above are highly uncertain and will depend on facts of a given case and the court's interpretation. For example, having in mind the intrinsic characteristic of unfair competition law, namely its flexibility, this area of law should not be deemed as a reliant legal mean sufficient to address the issues at the heart of the socialistic brands dilemma.

Socialistic brands subject to the 'abandonment scenario' should remain outside of the scope of trademark exclusivity. This ought not to be understood as synonymous to leaving these brands at the mercy of the wraith of the 'tragedy of the commons' – to be forgotten and to lose all their magnetism. The availability of these signs will encourage undertakings to use these highly attractive symbols in different ways, for example to offer replicas or other inspired commodities. As such commodities would be subject to competition, since anyone could use these 'free' socialistic brands, entities producing them would have to rely more on the quality and other characteristics of the commodities and not on the socialistic brand itself.

VI. A brand new nostalgia? Case examples touch-down.

Let us briefly come back to the case studies in order to access them in the light of the findings presented.

It seems that the case of Unitra[200] constitutes an instance in which registration of the trademark corresponding to a socialistic brand should be allowed as the proprietor of the mark seems to be a direct successor of the socialist enterprise.

Unlike Unitra, from the information gathered, it seems that the re-registration of Pewex is likely a case of unjustifiable appropriation of a socialist brand. There is no succession in this case. Thus, trademark registration constituted an unfair appropriation of the exclusivity over the sign. What is more, it is possible that the actions of launching the brand first as a user content driven platform for sharing images of other socialistic brands, including these, which are currently protected as trademarks, constitutes a tort of unfair competition.

In case of Herbapol it seems that there are legitimate grounds for all of the entities to be entitled to use the collective mark. However, the manner in which this sign is being currently used leads to consumer confusion and therefore this conduct is very likely against unfair competition law.

PTNS Finally, one might ask if all of the findings presented in this thesis imply that undertakings with no connection to socialism are unable to obtain exclusivity over signs characterised by magnetism evoking an authentic feeling of nostalgia for the socialist era. Pan Tu Nie Stał is a prime example that creating a new and yet 'authentically' nostalgic brand is possible. This privately-owned Polish clothing SME offers products with both original and inspired artworks that evoke nostalgia for the socialist era. The brand owners cooperate with designers from the socialist period on fair terms – part of profit from every sale of the Działka Moje Hobby t-shirt goes to the artist who designed the cover of the original book[201]. The example of the said t-shirt shows that signs belonging to the group of socialistic brands can be commercially re-used

---

200 National no. of the right: 60578.
201 *Supra* n. 106.

in a way that does not disrupt competition. The owners of Pan Tu Nie Stał were able to secure a copyright license from the creator, which conveys upon them a different type of exclusivity than that which would be conveyed on the basis of trademark law. A type of exclusivity that due to its nature is, ironically one might add, much better suited for signs the attractiveness of which has been shaped by the uncontrolled actions of end users rather than the actions sanctioned and controlled by their proprietor. Furthermore, Pan Tu Nie Stał employs national and regional sentiment through indicating that its products have been designed and manufactured in the Polish city of Łódź. This is a particularly important fact as Łódź is widely known as the centre of the textile industry of socialist Poland. Owners of Pan Tu Nie Stał have created a brand with its own unique magnetism by relying on cultural connotations and thus succeeded in creating a new nostalgia brand that plays off the heritage of socialism. This is a proof that there is no need to appropriate a socialistic brand for a new brand to gain an authentic relation with the times of socialism. Pan Tu Nie Stał is a registered national word mark as of 2013[202].

---

202 National no. of the right: 272274.

VII. Conclusion

Socialistic brands are a unique group of signs that have gained substantial 'selling power' through use in peculiar historical circumstances. Numerous instances of use of socialistic brands and their successful registrations as trademarks, show that there is a strong interest in them. As the omnipresence of emotional branding accelerates the process of blurring the line between the cultural meaning and commercial meaning of signs, driving changes to the nature of trademarks, undertakings show a strong preference towards brands that are characterised by unique magnetism. Socialistic brands, due to their historical pedigree and unique cultural connotations, possess strong and unique magnetism, which gives them substantial advantage over other signs. This magnetism spurs from the collective use of the signs rather than from the efforts of past or current proprietors. This unique magnetism translates to the value of these brands and thus to the value of the commodities affixed with them. An undertaking unjustifiably appropriating such signs would unfairly gain a substantial advantage over competitors. This advantage would not be gained through actions that could be attributed to efforts of the registrant other than a savvy business decision made to appropriate a socialistic brand. Allowing for such unjustifiable registration lowers the overall incentives for investment in the quality of products, as the magnetism of the socialistic brands spurs not from the efforts of an owner who has unjustifiably appropriated it but rather from their historical pedigree. Due to strong cultural meaning of these brands, an undertaking which unfairly appropriates a socialistic brand would be in a uniquely advantageous position to benefit from various social phenomenon. Because of a potentially perpetual term of protection as trademarks, socialistic brands could be re-launched numerous times, benefiting from such phenomenon as the minority effect.

Although the currently applicable law offers many provisions that could be evoked against cases of unfair appropriation of the socialistic brands, it does not constitute a satisfying mean of addressing the issue in a comprehensive way. This situation could be improved if governments of post-socialist countries, their courts and the relevant national agencies would recognise the public policy interest in keeping these cultural signs outside of the scope of trademark exclusivity.

An unjustifiable appropriation of a socialistic brand could perhaps be best visualised by evoking the following example. Let us imagine a socialistic brand as a type of inherently open and communal park. Due to the very nature of this park (sign within a culture) it cannot be sustained only by actions of its creators. Its existence and growth relies on its use by others. These others take some plants with them while leaving new behind, threading on some flowers whilst caring for others. The location of the park within the topography of a culture is as much determined by where it was originally created, as it is by the changes in its neighbouring plots and its neighbourhood in general. Due to its unique collectively shaped properties (use in unique historical circumstances), even if this particular park was abandoned by its creators, others won't cease visiting, caring for and changing it. This park can be used for many purposes and due to its unique location and content, it is likely to attract visitors for many years to come. However, it may be appealing for trademark proprietors, trademark law was not crated in order to facilitate 'remonopolisation' of something that re-proprietors cannot logically be entitled to. Namely, a meaning conveying unique magnetism, created by a given community within a given culture and not one single proprietor. Allowing for such unjustifiable appropriation of socialistic brands constitutes use of trademark law in a manner contrary to its very purpose and its competitive-neutral nature.

List of Works Cited

All sources consulted are cited in accordance with the Oxford University Standard for the Citation of Legal Authorities and The Guide To Polish Legal Citation.

Oxford University Standard for the Citation of Legal Authorities (4th edn, Hart 2012) <http://www.law.ox.ac.uk/published/OSCOLA_4th_edn_Hart_2012.pdf>.

Guide to Polish Legal Citation (JU-CUA American Law Program 2009) <http://www.law.uj.edu.pl/~citations/>.

Monographies and Articles

"Study on the Overall Functioning of the European Trade Mark System" (Max Planck Institute for Innovation and Competition Law Munich 2011) <http://www.ip.mpg.de/fileadmin/user_upload/mpi_final_report.pdf>.

George A. Akerlof, "The Market for 'Lemons': Quality Uncertainty and the Market Mechanism" (1970) 84 Quarterly Journal of Economics 3, 488.

Katya Assaf, "The dilution of Culture and the Law of trademarks" (2009) 49 IDEA – The intellectual Property Law Review 1 <http://ssrn.com/abstractc=1410590>.

J. Barta, „Przeszkody w Rejestracji" Janusz Barta, Ryszard Markiewicz & Andrzej Matlak (eds); *Prawo Mediów* (LexisNexis 2008).

Roland Barthes, Adam Dziadek (tr) "Imperium Znaków" (eng."Empire of Signs"), (Aletheia 2012).

Roland Barthes, Richard Howard (tr) "Camera Lucida: Reflections on Photography" (Farrar, Straus and Giroux 1981).

Mikhail Bakhtin, Vadim Liapunov (tr), Michael Holquist & Vadim Liapunov (eds) "Art and Answerability" (Austin University of Texas Press 1990).

Mikhail Bakhtin, Vern W. McGee (tr), Caryl Emerson and Michael Holquist (eds) "Speech Genresand, Other Late Essays" (University of Texas Press 2006).

Burton Beebe, "The Semiotic Analysis of Trademark Law" (2004) 51 UCLA Law Rev. 3, 621.

Burton Beebe, "The Semiotic Account of Trademark Doctrine and Trademark Culture", Graeme Dimwoodie, Mark Jamis (eds), *Trademark Law and Theory: A Handbook of Contemporary Research* (Cheltenham 2008).

Daphne Berdahl, "'(N)Ostalgie' for the Present: Memory, Longing, and East German Things" (1999) 64 Ethnos 2, 193.

Edward L. Bernays, "Biography of an Idea: Memoirs of Public Relations Counsel" (Simon and Schuster 1965).

Jason Bosland, "The Culture of Trade Marks: An Alternative Cultural Theory Perspective" (2005) 10 Media & Arts Law Review 99.

Laura R. Bradford, "Trademark dilution and emotion" <http://papers.ssrn.com/sol3/pa pers.cfm?abstract_id=1334925&download=yes>.

Valerie Brennan, T.J. Crane "Gone But Not Goodbye: Residual Goodwill in Aban-doned U.S. Trademarks" (Inta Bulletin, 15.8.2015) <http://www.inta.org/INTABull etin/Pages/GoneButNotGoodbyeResidualGoodwillinAbandonedUSTrademarks.asp x>.

Jan M. Broekman, Larry Catá Backer (eds) "Signs In Law – A Source Book The Semi-otics of Law in Legal Education III" (Springer 2015).

Rosemary J. Coombe, "Embodied Trademarks: Mimesis and Alterity on American Commercial Frontiers" (1996) 11 Cultural Anthropology 2, 202.

Norman Davis, "God's Playground: A History of Poland: 1795 to the Present (Volume 2)" (2nd edn, Oxford University Press 2005).

Graeme Dinwoodie, "Reconceptualizing the Inherent Distinctiveness of Product Design Trade Dress" (1997) 75 North Carolina Law Review 2, 471.

Jennifer Davis "Between a Sign and a Brand", L. Bently, Jennifer Davis & J.C. Gins-burg (eds) *Trademarks and Brands* (Cambridge 2008), 65.

Kristofer Erickson, Paul Heald, Fabian Homberg, Martin Kretschmer and Dinusha Mendis, "Copyright and the Value of the Public Domain" (CREATe 2015) <http://w ww.create.ac.uk/publications/copyright-and-the-value-of-the-public-domain/>.

Jerome Gilson, Anne Gilson LaLonde, "The Zombie Trademark: A Windfall and A Pitfall"(2006) 98 Trademark Reporter 6, 1280.

Matt Haig, "Brand Royalty: How the World's Top 100 Brands Thrive & Survive" (Kogan Page Publishers, 2006).

Susy Frankel, "Trademarks and Traditional Knowledge and Cultural Intellectual Prop-erty Rights", 1 Victoria University of Wellington Legal Research Papers 6, <http://p apers.ssrn.com/abstract=1003608>.

William M. Landes, Richard A. Posner, "The Economics of Trademark Law" (1988), 78 The Trademark Reporter 3, 267.

Peter Kelvin, "Book Review: Social Influence and Social Change by Serge Moscovic" (1979) 9 European Journal of Social Psychology, 441.

Janusz Szwaja (red.) „Ustawa o zwalczaniu nieuczciwej konkurencji Komentarz" (3rd ed. C.H.Beck 2013).

Philip Kotler, "Marketing Insights from A to Z" (John Wiley & Sons, Inc. 2003).

Piotr Kozarzewski, "Corporate Governance and Secondary Privatisation in Poland: Legal Framework and Changes in Ownership Structure" (Center for Social and Economic Research 2003) <http://ssrn.com/abstract=1443803> accesed on 15 September 2015.

Michał Kruk, "Protection of Chopin's Heritage as a Sui Generis Regulation" (2010), 5 Journal of Intellectual Property Law & Practice 8, 608.

Paul Manning, "The Semiotics of Brand" (2010) The Annual Review of Anthropology 39, 33.

Mark P. McKenna, "A Consumer Decision-Making Theory of Trademark Law" (2012) 98 Virginia Law Review 1, 67.

Anne Meneley, "Time in a Bottle: The Uneasy Circulation of Palestinian Olive Oil" (2008) Middle East Reporter 248, <http://www.academia.edu/474517/Time_in_a_B ottle_The_Uneasy_Circulation_of_Palestinian_Olive_Oil>, 18.

B. Mercurio, "Awakening the Sleeping Giant: Intellectual Property Right in International Investment Agreement" (2012) 15 J Int Economic Law 3, 874.

Robert Moore, "From Genericide to Viral Marketing: on 'Brand'" (2003) Language & Communication 23, 334.

Serge Moscovici, Maria Zavalloni, "The Group as a Polarizer of Attitudes" (1969) 12 Journal of Personality and Social Psychology 2, 125.

Serge Moscovici, "Social Influence and Social Change" (Academic Press 1976).

Serge Moscovici, "Toward a Theory of Conversion Behaviour", Leonard Berkowitz (eds), *Advances in Experimental Social Psychology, vol 13* (Academic Press 1980).

Charlan Jeanne Nemeth, „The Differential Contributions of Majority and Minority Influence" (1986) 93 Psychological Review 1, 23.

Charlan Jeanne Nemeth, „Minority Influence Theory", Paul A. M. Van Lange, Arie W. Kruglanski, E. Tory Higgins (eds), *Handbook of Theories in Social Psychology vol 2* (Sage 2011).

Ewa Nowińska, Michał du Vall „Pojęcie Złej Wiary w Prawie Znaków Towarowych" in *Księga Pamiątkowa z Okazji 85-lecia Ochrony Własności Przemysłowej w Polsce*, 143.

Charles Sanders Peirce in Charles Hartshorne and Paul Weiss (eds) "Collected Papers of Charles Sanders Peirce: Vol. II, Elements of Logic" (Belknap Press 1932), 228.

Ferdinand de Saussure, Weds Baskins (tr.), Charles Bally and Albert Sechehaye (eds.) "Course in General Linguistics" (1966 McGraw-Hill Book Co), 112.

Wolgang Sakulin, *Trademark Protection and Freedom of Expression: An Inquiry Into the Conflict Between Trademark Rights and Freedom of Expression Under European Law* (Kluwer Law International, 2011).

Frank I. Schechter "The rational basis of trademark protection" (1927) 40 Harv. Law Rev. 6, 813.

Jonathan E. Schroeder, "Brand Culture: Trade Marks, Marketing and Consumption" in Jane Ginsburg, Lionel Bently & Jennifer Davis (eds) *Trade Marks and Brands An Interdisciplinary Critique* (Cambridge University Press 2008), 174.

Martin Senftleben, "Bringing EU Trademark Protection Back Into Shape – Lessons to Learn From Keyword Advertising", <http://www.epip.eu/conferences/epip06/paper s/Parallel%20Session%20Papers/SENFTLEBEN%20Martin.pdf>.

Martin Senftleben, „Trademark Law and the Public Domain" <http://papers.ssrn.com/s ol3/papers.cfm?abstract_id=2280058>.

Johnathan E. Shroeder, "Brand Culture: Trade Marks, Marketing and Consumption" in L. Bently, Jennifer Davis & J.C. Ginsburg (eds) *Trademarks and Brands* (Cambridge 2008), 161.

Ryszard Skubisz (eds.), „System Prawa Prywatnego tom 14b Prawo własności Przemysłowej" (C·H·Beck 2012).

Ryszard Skubisz, „Zgłoszenie Znaku Towarowego w Złej Wierze" in L. Ogiegło, W. Popiołek, M. Szpunar (red.) *Rozprawy prawnicze, Księga pamiątkowa Profesora Maksymiliana Pazdana* (Kraków 2005), 1342.

Alexander Tsoutsanis, "Trade Mark Registration In Bad Faith" (Oxford 2010).

Press articles and others

"Horalky Budú Vyrábať Opavia – LU aj I.D.C. Holding" (*finance.sk*, 12.4.2006) <http://www.finance.sk/spravy/finance/4993-horalky-budu-vyrabat-opavia-lu-aj-i-d-c-holding/>.

"Dohoda o Používaní Názvu Horalka a Tatranka Více" (*Strategie.cz*, 8.11.2007) <http://strategie.e15.cz/zpravy/dohoda-o-pouzivani-nazvu-horalka-a-tatranka-44364 3>.

Saul McLeod "Moscovici and Minority Influence" (*Simple Psychology*, 2007) <www.simplypsychology.org/minority-influence.html>.

Marta Karenova, "Soviet-Era Brands Rise On Socialist Nostalgia" (*Wall Street Journal* 15.11.2004), <http://www.wsj.com/articles/SB110046692372873477>.

Sergei Roganov, „Soviet Food Passes Taste Test for New Generation" (*Rossiyskaya Gazeta, Telegraph* 3.1.2013) <http://www.telegraph.co.uk/sponsored/rbth/cuisine/9 778200/soviet-food-popular.html>.

Official European Union profile of Poland <http://europa.eu/about-eu/countries/memb er-countries/poland/index_en.htm>.

Dawid Kosiński, „Unitra – kultowa polska marka powraca na rynek i oferuje produkty "born in Poland"" (*Spider's web*, 22.5.2014) <http://www.spidersweb.pl/2014/05/un itra-wraca-na-rynek.html>.

"Pewex Wraca na Rynek" (*Rzeczpospolita Ekonomia,* 16.12.2013) <http://www.ekono mia.rp.pl/artykul/1072971.html>.

Ewa Cander-Karolewska, „Atlantyda Ludowa" (*Onet wiadomości*, 1.07.2007) <http:// wiadomosci.onet.pl/prasa/atlantyda-ludowa/dxxm3>.

Grzegorz Marczak, „Dlaczego Chłopaki z Pruszcza Chcą Reaktywować Pewex? Na Moje Pytania Odpowiedział Sebastian Leśniak" (*Antyweb* 7.6.2013)< http://antywe b.pl/dlaczego-chlopaki-z-pruszcza-chca-reaktywowac-pewex-na-moje-pytania-odpo wiedzial-sebastian-lesniak/>.

Ꮩուֆ «Գրանֆ Ֆեֆֆ» ёш°ⱨ ६Ŧ ՍԲրֆ (*168 ժամ,* 24.10.2015) <http://archive.168.am/am/ar ticles/20366>.

Results for "Działka Moje Hobby" in the Polish National Library catalogue <http://kat alogi.bn.org.pl/iii/encore/search/C__Sdzia>.

"Tíz Régi Magyar Márka – Emlékszünk-e Még Rájuk" (*hvg.hu*, 8.7.2011) < http://hvg. hu/tudomany/20110707_regi_magyar_marka>.

"Az Adidas Cipők is a Tiszánál Készültek" (*haszonkulcs.hu*, 7.12.2011) <http://archive -hu-2012.com/hu/h/2012-06-21_62606_12/Sikert%C3%B6rt%C3%A9netek-Az-Ad idas-cip%C5%91k-is-a-Tisz%C3%A1n%C3%A1l-k%C3%A9sz%C3%BCltek-Has zonkulcs/>.

Official announcement of the Biedronka launch of the vintage assortment <http://www.biedronka.pl/pl/news,id,877,title,biedronka-zaprasza-w-podroz-sentymentalna-z-produktami-vintage>.

Mikołaj Lech, „Po 58 Latach Wedel Odzyskuje Prawo do Nazwy "PTASIE MLECZKO"" (*Wyborcza biz*, 10.11.2014) <http://wyborcza.biz/Prawo/1,128894,16946756,Po_58_latach_Wedel_odzyskuje_prawo_do_nazwy__PTASIE.html>.

Artur Kawik, „Walka o „Ptasie Mleczko®" Przyczyną Kryzysu Wizerunkowego Wedla" (*Socialpress* 13.2.2012) < http://socialpress.pl/2012/02/walka-o-ptasie-mleczko-przyczyna-kryzysu-wizerunkowego-wedla/>.

"Ce au in Comun Automobile Dacia si Arctic Gaesti: Ambele Businessuri Sunt Sustinute de Campaniile „Rabla" si Exporturi" (*ZF Companii*, 26.8.2009) <http://www.zf.ro/companii/ce-au-in-comun-automobile-dacia-si-arctic-gaesti-ambele-businessuri-sunt-sustinute-de-campaniile-rabla-si-exporturi-4801812/>.

Robert Mazurek, "Świat Miał Wranglery, My – Dżinsy Odra" (*Rzeczpospolita* 14.8.2015) <http://www.rp.pl/artykul/1222410-Swiat-mial-Wranglery--my---dzinsy-Odra.html>.

Daria Różańska, „Twórcy Demotywatory.pl Wprowadzają do Sieci Markę Pewex" (*press.pl*, 17.12.2013) <http://www.press.pl/personalia/pokaz/43761,Tworcy-Demotywatory_pl-wprowadzaja-do-sieci-marke-Pewex>.

Unitra official page, <http://unitra.pl/>.

Unitra club, <http://unitraklub.pl/unitra-dom>.

Unitra – official facebook page <https://www.facebook.com/unitrapl>.

Herbapol Poznań < http://www.herbapol.poznan.pl/historia>.

Herbapol Lublin < http://www.herbapol.com.pl/o-nas/kim-jestesmy>.

Herbapol w Krakowie < http://herbapol.krakow.pl/o-firmie/historia>.

Herbapol Warszawa <http://www.herbapol.waw.pl/>

Herbapol Wrocła < http://herbapol.pl/>.

Ursus official page <http://en.ursus.com.pl/History>.

Official Wedel page <https://www.wedelpijalnie.pl/pl/o-nas/e-wede>.

Legislation

Council Regulation (EC) 207/2009/EC on the Community trade mark (codified version) [2009] OJ L78/1.

Council Directive (EC) 2008/95/EC to approximate the laws of the Member States relating to trade marks (codified version) [1993] OJ L299/25.

Polish Industrial Property Act – Ustawa z dnia 30 czerwca 2000 r. Prawo własności przemysłowej, Dz.U. 2001 nr 49 poz. 508 with changes.

Cases

EU

Case C- 106/89 *Marleasing SA v La Comercial* EU:C:1990:395, [1990] ECR I-4135.

Case C-363/99 *Koninklijke KPN Nederland NV v. Benelux-Merkenbureau* EU:C: 2004:86, [2004] ECR I-1619.

Case C-329/02 SAT. 1 *SatellitenFernsehen GmbH v. OHIM* EU:C:2004:532, [2004] ECR I-08317.

Case C-320/12 *Malaysia Diary Industries Pte. Ltd v. Ankenaevnet for Petendter og Varemaerk* EU:C:2013:435.

Case C-487/07 *L'Oréal SA v. Bellure NV* EU:C:2009:378, [2009] ECR I-05185.

Case C-108/05 *Bovemij Verzekeringen v. Benelux-Merkenbureau* EU:C:2006:530, [2006] ECR I-07605.

Case C-265/00 *Campina Melkunie BV v Benelux* EU:C:2004:87, [2004] ECR I-01699.

Cases C-53/01 and C-55/01 *Linde and others* EU:C:2003:206, [2003] ECG I-03161.

Case T-304/06 *Reber v OHMI* EU:T:2008:268, [2008] ECG II-01927.

Case C-383/99 P *Procter & Gamble* EU:C:2001:461, [2001] ECG I-06251.

Case C-529/07 *Chocoladenfabriken Lindt & Sprüngli* EU:C:2009:361, [2009] EGC I-04893.

Case C-17/06 *Celine* EU:C:2007:497, [2007] EGC I-07041.

Case C-408/01 *Adidas v. Salomon* EU:C:2003:582, [2003] EGC I-12558.

Poland

Judgement of NSA of 12.7.2011, II GSK 746/10.

Judgment of NSA of 14.1.2015, II GSK 1815/14.

Judgment of NSA of 24.5.2007, II GSK 377/06.

Judgements of NSA of 25.5.2006, II GSK 66/06.

Judgements of NSA of 8.1.2014, II GSK 1542/12.

Judgement of NSA of 24.5.2005, II GSK 63/05.

Judgement of NSA of 4.6.2002, II SA 3867/01.

Judgement of NSA of 25.11.2009, II GSK 203/09.

Judgement of NSA of 9.1.2015 II GSK 2062/13.

Jusgement of WSA in Warsaw of 5.9.2014, VI SA/Wa 1995/13.

Jusgement of WSA in Warsaw of 29.5.2014 VI SA/Wa 1996/13.

Jusgement of WSA in Warsaw of 29.5.2014 VI SA/Wa 1980/13.

Judgement of WSA in Warsaw of 7.1.2014, VI SA/Wa 1716/13.

Judgement of WSA in Warszawie of 18.1.2012 r, VI SA/Wa 1850/11.

Judgement of WSA in Warsaw of 21.3.2012, VI SA/Wa 1761/06.

Judgement of WSA in Warsaw of 14.6.2013, VI Sa/Wa 101/13.

Judgement of the Court of Appeals in Warsaw of 6.11.2015 I ACz 1640/12.

Judgement of the Supreme Court of 24.10.1972, I CR 177/72, (OSNCP 10/73, p. 171).

Judgements of the Supreme Court of 12.10.2007, V CSK 249/07 (OSG 2009, 4, 25).

Judgement of the Supreme Court of 14.2.2003, IV CKN 1782/00 (LexPolonica 379001).

Judgement of the Supreme Court of 10.8.2006, V CSK 237/06.

Other jurisdictions

Anheuser-Busch Inc v Portugal, Merits, App no 73049/01, (2007) 44 EHRR 42, IHRL 3436 (ECHR 2007).

Judgement of the Dutch Supreme Court of 20.12.2013, 12/05013 TT/AS.